高等学校"十二五"规划教材
市政与环境工程系列丛书

Professional English for Environmental Science and Engineering

环境科学与工程专业英语

主编 潘 宇 钟子楠
主审 宋志伟

内 容 简 介

本书由专业英语翻译理论、专业英语阅读和专业英语写作3部分组成,这3个部分在结构上相互联系、有机结合,在内容安排上具有较强的逻辑性、系统性和实用性。第1部分着重讲述了英译汉的基本方法和技巧,为读者阅读专业文献搭建平台;第2部分精选了6个单元14篇与环境专业密切相关的阅读文章,语言规范,内容新颖,信息量大;第3部分主要介绍了英语科技论文的写作方法,并列举代表性强的环境科学及工程领域的科技论文作为范例,为读者阅读专业文献提供了完备性的指导。

本书可作为高等学校环境科学和环境工程专业本科生及研究生专业英语课程教材,对于科技工作者和其他相关专业学生提高专业英语的阅读、翻译和写作水平也有重要参考价值。

图书在版编目(CIP)数据

环境科学与工程专业英语/潘宇,钟子楠主编—哈尔滨:哈尔滨工业大学出版社,2015.8(2022.7重印)
ISBN 978-7-5603-5552-8

Ⅰ.①环… Ⅱ.①潘… ②钟… Ⅲ.①环境科学-英语-高等学校-教材②环境工程-英语-高等学校-教材 Ⅳ.①H31

中国版本图书馆 CIP 数据核字(2015)第 181224 号

策划编辑	贾学斌
责任编辑	郭 然
出版发行	哈尔滨工业大学出版社
社　　址	哈尔滨市南岗区复华四道街 10 号　邮编 150006
传　　真	0451-86414749
网　　址	http://hitpress.hit.edu.cn
印　　刷	哈尔滨圣铂印刷有限公司
开　　本	787mm×1092mm　1/16　印张 10.25　字数 220 千字
版　　次	2015 年 8 月第 1 版　2022 年 7 月第 4 次印刷
书　　号	ISBN 978-7-5603-5552-8
定　　价	36.00 元

(如因印装质量问题影响阅读,我社负责调换)

前　言

环境科学与工程专业英语课程是高等院校环境专业教育的重要组成部分,是提高学生环境意识及国际学术交流的基础,通过专业英语的学习,可以提升学生专业英语翻译与交流能力、专业论文摘要与论文撰写能力。

本书由专业英语翻译理论、专业英语阅读和专业英语写作3部分组成。第1部分着重讲述了英译汉的基本方法和技巧,列举了大量有代表性的例句,并对其中的长句、难句进行了详细的分析,目的是使学生很好地实现从大学基础英语到科技英语的过渡,掌握一定的科技文章的翻译技巧,为读者阅读专业文献做铺垫。第2部分精选了6个单元14篇与环境专业密切相关的阅读文章,内容主要包括目前的环境状况和主要环境经济问题,水污染的基本知识以及水污染防治技术,微生物相关知识及其在废水处理中的作用,主要的大气污染现象及对人类的影响,固体废物的种类及其处理等相关知识,使学生在掌握专业词汇的同时能够对环境专业知识有一个系统的了解。第3部分主要介绍了英语科技论文的写作方法,并列举代表性强的环境科学及工程领域的科技论文作为范例,目的是使学生掌握专业写作的方法,增强阅读英文文献和用英文表达研究及成果的能力。

本书由潘宇负责全书的构思及第1~6,8,9,11,12章的编写;钟子楠负责第7,10,13章的编写。全书由宋志伟主审。

本书在编写和出版过程中,得到了黑龙江科技大学青年才俊专项基金的资助和宋志伟教授的大力支持和帮助,在此表示衷心的感谢!

由于作者水平有限,书中难免存在疏漏和不妥之处,敬请读者批评指正。

编　者
2015年5月

Contents

Part 1 Translation Skills ... 1

Chapter 1 Word Features and Translation skills ... 3

1.1 Word Features ... 3

1.2 The Skills in the Translation of Words ... 4

Chapter 2 Transformation of Sentence Constituents ... 7

2.1 Transformation of Adverbial to Subject ... 7

2.2 Transformation of Object to Subject ... 8

2.3 Transformation of Predicative to Subject ... 9

2.4 Transformation of Attribute to Subject ... 9

2.5 Transformation of Predicate to Subject ... 10

2.6 Transformation of Subject to Predicate ... 10

2.7 Transformation of Predicative to Predicate ... 10

2.8 Transformation of Attribute to Predicate ... 11

2.9 Transformation of Adverbial to Attribute ... 11

2.10 Transformation of Subject to Object ... 12

2.11 Transformation of Attribute to Adverbial ... 12

  2.12 Transformation of Adverbial to Complement ················· 13

Chapter 3 Adjustment of Word and Sentence Order ················· 14

  3.1 Adjustment of Word Order ················· 14

  3.2 Adjustment of Sentence Order ················· 18

Chapter 4 Translation of Passive Voice ················· 21

  4.1 Translation to Active Sentence ················· 21

  4.2 Translation to Passive Sentence ················· 23

  4.3 Translation to Sentence with No Subject ················· 23

Chapter 5 Translation of Attributive Clause ················· 25

  5.1 Translation of Restrictive Clause ················· 25

  5.2 Translation of Non-restrictive Clause ················· 28

Part 2 Reading ················· 33

Chapter 6 The Environment and Environmental Issues ················· 35

  6.1 What is "The Environment" ················· 35

  6.2 Global Environmental Issues ················· 37

Chapter 7 Environmental Economics ················· 40

  7.1 What is Environmental Economics ················· 40

  7.2 Concepts ················· 40

  7.3 Solutions ················· 41

Chapter 8   Water Pollution 44

8.1   Water Pollution Problems 44

8.2   Sewage Treatment 46

Chapter 9   Microorganisms 53

9.1   Biological Components of Sewage 53

9.2   Anaerobic Digestion 57

Chapter 10   Air Pollution 60

10.1   Air Pollution Problems 60

10.2   Air Pollutants 63

10.3   Effects of Air Pollution on Human Health 66

Chapter 11   Solid Waste 82

11.1   Solid Waste Problems 82

11.2   Treatment and Disposal of Municipal Waste 85

Part 3   Writing 89

Chapter 12   The Abstract 91

12.1   The Abstract and Its Function 91

12.2   The Classification of Abstract 92

12.3   The Abstract Writing 100

Chapter 13   Scientific Paper 104

13.1	Title	105
13.2	Author	107
13.3	Introduction	108
13.4	Materials and Methods	115
13.5	Results and Discussion	124
13.6	Conclusion	143
13.7	Acknowledgments	146
13.8	References	147

References 155

Part 1　Translation Skills

Chapter 1　Word Features and Translation Skills

1.1　Word Features

科技英语是在普通英语基础之上发展起来的,因此无论是在词汇方面还是在语法方面,与基础英语没有绝对的界限。但科技英语语言在发展的长期过程中逐渐形成了自己的特色。

1. 科技英语词汇

科技英语词汇由 3 部分组成:普通词汇(common words)、半技术词汇(semi-technical words)和专业词汇(specialized terms)。其中普通词汇占绝大部分,尤其是环境工程专业英语。半技术词汇也是普通词汇,不过在不同学科中具有不同的意义。以 power 为例,普通含义为权力、能力;在数学上其含义是幂或乘方,例如:X^n,读作 X to the power nth/ the nth power of X;在物理学上其含义是功率,例如:horsepower。专业词汇在科技英语中仅占很少一部分,较为难记,但意义单一,用法稳定。例如:eutrophication,释义:If it happens in the lakes or rivers, we call it water bloom; If it happens in the seas or oceans, we call it red tide.

2. 缩写词

COD　BOD　DO　TOC　TOD　TSP　TP　PM10　PM2.5　POPs

3. 句子

科技英语句子较长,但句型变化较少,关系代词 that,which 以及非人称代词使用频率高。

1.2　The Skills in the Translation of Words

1.2.1　To select and determine the meaning of a word

英语中的单词根据词义通常可分为两大类:单义词和多义词。其中单义词很少,90%以上属于多义词。一般专业词汇较多为多义词。多义词包含两个方面:含义有多个;词性有多个。因而,在翻译过程中需要进行正确的词义选择。一般从以下几个方面着手。

1. Subject

n. 题目;问题;主题;学科;科目等
adj. 受他人统治的;未独立的;倾向于;易于;服从于,受某事物支配;取决于
v. 征服,制服;经历或遭受某事物 subject sb. / sth. to sth.

例如:Organic substances are subject to slow attack by oxygen on exposure to air. 暴露于空气中的有机物质容易受到氧的缓慢氧化。It is known to all that the subject of electronics was born from radio. 众所周知,电子学这门学科是从无线电学衍生而来的。It is necessary to subject the metal to great heat. 必须给这种金属加高热。As a test, the metal was subjected to great heat. 这种金属经受住了高热试验。Most of the bodies around us are subject to several forces. 我们周围的大部分固体都受到几个力的作用。

2. Light

n. 光;光线;电灯;火柴;打火机
v. 点火;照亮
adj. 轻的;不重的
adv. 淡;轻便

例如:Light travels faster than sound. 光的传播速度比声音快。All light may be traced to the sun. The sun lights our world even in dark. 所有的光都来源于太阳。即使在黑夜太阳仍旧照亮我们的世界。Uranium – 235 is slightly lighter than Uranium – 238. 铀235比铀238稍轻一些。The experience show that any object submerged in water seems to be lighter. 经验表明浸没在水中的任何物体看起来都要轻一些。Turn on the light. 打开灯。Strike a light, please. 请打个火。Don't make light of their design. 不要轻视他们的设计。These facts throw light on the subject. 这些事实使问题清楚了。You should travel light. 你应该轻装旅行。

1.2.2 Variation in the number of words

1. An addition to the number of words

在科技英语翻译中,根据句法结构和修饰效果的需要,词的增译通常有以下3种情况:首先,增译的一些词在英语原文中虽无其形但是有其义;第二,有些词在英语中可以省略而不影响全句意义的完整表达,但是若在汉语译文中省略了,就会发生表达意义不明确、译文不通顺的问题;第三,尽管有些词在英语惯用语法上是意思明确而完整的,但逐词译成汉语后,就会使全句意义不够清楚、译文难以理解。因此,汉语译文增译词语是为了使译文意义更加流畅、明确和通顺。

在翻译中,某些表示动作意义的名词在表示具体概念时往往需要补充汉语名词,如作用、效应、方法、方式、技术、过程等。He was equally at home with the abstractions of number theory, the long calculations of astronomy and the practicalities of applied physics. 他对数论的抽象性,对天文的冗长的计算方法以及对应用物理学的实际应用问题都是同样精通的。

汉语补充名词以使英语动词的意义更加明确完整。Television enables us to see at a distance far beyond the range of the human eye. 电视能够使我们看到远远超出我们人眼能看到的范围以外的东西。

汉语补充英语中省略的词以使译文更加通顺。We obtained monomolecular rather than bimolecular compounds. 我们得到的是单分子化合物而不是双分子化合物。

2. The subtraction from the number of words

如同词的增译一样,科技英语翻译中词的省译是常见的,这是由于英、汉两种语言表达方式不同造成的。例如,英语中经常使用冠词,而汉语中没有冠词,如果逐词死译,可能累赘甚至不通顺,因为有些介词、连词、代词等是不必要翻译出来的。但是要记住一点,省译不是任意删改英语原文的意思,而是要在不歪曲原文内容的前提下使译文的内容言简意赅、通顺地道。

(1) To leave out English articles in translation 冠词的省译

冠词在英语中很常用,但是有不少是没有意义的,故可省略。但是翻译时必须注意那些使词组意义发生改变的冠词。例如:a carpenter must know how to use a power saw. 木匠必须知道如何使用电锯。

(2) To leave out English prepositions in translation 介词的省译

英语中介词使用很频繁,例如:Sounds having the same frequency are in resonance. 具有相同频率的声音会共振。

(3) To leave out some English pronouns in translation 代词的省译

最常见的就是 it。例如:It is important to apply the results of scientific researches to production. 把科研成果应用于生产中是很重要的。

3. The extension of the meaning of a word or a phrase

由于英、汉两种语言在表达上有许多差异,有时很难从词典中找到一个与原意相当适合的词义。因此,必须仔细考虑上下文的逻辑关系,原文的历史等,将一个词或是一个句子从基本词义出发进行必要的引申。例如:The earthquake occurs when the rocks are strained to fissure. 当岩石拉伸到断裂时就会发生地震。Today is the link between yesterday and tomorrow. 今天是昨天和明天的桥梁。

4. Transformation of character speech

在翻译过程中,不能机械地按照原来的词性翻译,可根据汉语习惯进行词性的转换。例如:Neutrons act differently from protons. 中子的作用不同于质子。The main object of sedimentation is the separation of clear water from mixture. 沉淀的主要目的是将清水从混合液中分离出来。These data has been made use of in production. 生产中已利用了这些数据。We are not sure about the effect of this parameter on the quality of the effluent. 我们不能确定这个参数对出水水质的影响。This article aims at discussing new development in component material and technologies. 本文的目的在于讨论元件材料与技术的新进展。Oxygen is one of the important elements in the world, it is very active chemically. 氧是世界上的重要元素之一,它的化学性质很活泼。This communication system is chiefly characterized by its simplicity of operation and the ease with it can be maintained. 这种操作系统的主要特点是操作简单,易于维修。The table below shows the specific gravities of metals. 下表给出了各种金属的密度。

Chapter 2　Transformation of Sentence Constituents

由于英、汉两种语言的句子结构和表达方式不同，英译汉时，除了词类转译外，有时还需要转译句子成分，这是科技英语翻译常用的方法。事实上，词类的转换就意味着句子成分的转换。例如：当名词转换成动词或形容词时，该名词的语法功能相应地也就成为汉语的谓语、定语或状语。

2.1　Transformation of Adverbial to Subject

1. 在 There be 句型中，通常把句子中的状语译为主语

(1) There are different elements in the nature.

直译：在自然界中有许多种不同的元素。

转译：自然界中有许多种不同的元素。

相比之下，转译后的句子表达得更通顺、流畅。

(2) The device is shown schematically in Figure 8.

直译：在图 8 中显示出了这种装置的简图。

转译：这种装置的简图如图 8 所示。

2. 如果句子为被动语态，把句中的地点状语及由介词 for 或 by 引导的介词短语译成汉语的主语

(1) Heat and light can be given off by this chemical change. 这种化学反应能够放出光和热。

(2) Oxides of nitrogen are produced by combustion of organic matter. 有机物的燃烧产生氮氧化物。

(3) The same signs and symbols of mathematics are used throughout the world. 全世界都使用同样的数学符号。

3. 当句中的状语在意义上指和主语有关系的某一方面或某一位置时，有时可把这种状语译成主语，而把句中的真正主语译成定语（或者说是当介词短语修饰说明谓语动词

或表语时,将这一做状语的介词短语译成主语)

(1) These material are highly variable in nature. 句中的介词短语 in nature 为主语的某一方面性质(或用来修饰说明表语 variable),因此将它译为主语,原主语译为定语。这些物质的性质有很大差异。

(2) Atoms differ in weights because they contain different amount of matter. 介词短语 in weight 说明谓语动词 differ,与上句类似。原子的质量不同,因为它们含有不同量的物质。

(3) When water freezes, it becomes larger in volume instead of smaller. 水结冰时,它的体积变大而不是变小。

(4) These processes are very similar in principle. 这些工艺的原理十分相似。

4. 当英语中的副词译成汉语的名词时,有时将该副词译为主语

(1) The image must be dimensionally correct. 句中将副词 dimensionally 译为名词"尺寸"做主语。图形的尺寸必须正确。

(2) The equipment they have just developed is shown schematically in Figure 1. 他们刚研制出的设备简图如图 1 所示。

2.2 Transformation of Object to Subject

有些不表示动作而是表示主语所处特征的及物动词,如 have, produce, provide 等的宾语,有时可译成汉语的主语,这种译法主要是根据汉语的表达方式和表达习惯而定的,这样处理时,原句中的主语往往译成定语,谓语动词省去不译。

(1) LRCs have a lower sulphur content. 低阶煤的硫含量较低。

(2) Steam turbines provide a relatively small loss of energy. 汽轮机的能量损耗较小。

(3) Hot-set system produces higher strength than cold set-system. 热固系统比冷固系统的强度高。

在以上 3 个句子中,谓语动词 have, provide 和 produce 都不表示动作,而表示主语所处的状态,这样将宾语 sulphur, energy 和 strength 都译成主语,原主语 LRCs, steam turbines 和 hot-set system 都译成定语,而将做定语的形容词 lower, small 和 higher 译成谓语。

Chapter 2　Transformation of Sentence Constituents

2.3　Transformation of Predicative to Subject

1. 当表语是名词时,往往将该名词译成主语,此时原主语译成定语或表语(如果主语和表语在意思上一致,则将主语译成表语。如果表语是主语的某种属性,则将主语译成定语)

例如:The important problem that concern the economic development of our country is the production of iron and steel. 钢铁的生产是关系到我国经济发展的重要问题。One of the most important factors influencing the purification effect of waste water is turbidity. 浊度是影响废水净化的最重要的因素之一。Matter is anything which occupies space. 凡占有空间的东西都是物质。

在以上3个句子中,主语和表语在意思上都是一致的,因此将它们的主语和表语分别互换位置。

2. 表示事物特征的形容词做表语时,往往将这种形容词表语译成主语

例如:Ice is not as <u>dense</u> as water and therefore it floats. 冰的密度比水小,因此它在水中上浮。The more carbon the steel contains, the <u>harder and stronger</u> it is。钢中的碳含量越高,它的硬度和强度也就越大。

2.4　Transformation of Attribute to Subject

为了使译文的语言连贯,有时也将英语中的定语译为汉语的主语. 例如:There are three states <u>of matter</u>:solid,liquid and gas. 将句中的定语 of matter 译为主语。物质有三态:固态、液态和气态。The idea <u>of obtaining potable water from wastewater</u> is a psychologically difficult one for many people to accept. 对许多人来说,从污水中获得饮用水是一种在心理上难以接受的观念。A minimum of 1.5 to 2.0 milligrams/liter of <u>dissolved oxygen</u> is maintained in the aeration tank. 充氧槽内的溶解氧含量至少应保持在1.5~2.0 mg/L。

2.5　Transformation of Predicate to Subject

当动词译成名词时,该名词就随之转化成汉语的主语,不表示动作的动词,例如:act, result, differ, behave, feature 等,均应译成主语,而原来的主语译成定语(参看动词译成名词部分)。例如:This acid functions to kill bacteria in foods. 这种酸的作用是杀死食物中的细菌。His treatise aims at discussing the properties of the newly disovered elements. 他的论文的目的在于讨论新发现的各种元素的特性。

2.6　Transformation of Subject to Predicate

充当主语的名词译成动词时,常将此主语译成谓语。例如:The statement of the first law of motions as follows. 句中的名词 statement 译为动词"叙述",主语也相应地转译为谓语。运动第一定律叙述如下。Attempts are made to develop a new technique for denitrification. 将句中做主语的名词 attempts 转译为谓语动词"试图"。试图开发一种新的脱氮技术。Improvement of efficiency of the machine can be gained by reducing friction. 与上句类似,将 improvement 译为动词"提高"。减小摩擦,可以提高机械效率。The following definition apply to the terms used ln this specification. 此句中,可以将 definition 译为名词和动词的情况进行比较:译为名词,下述定义适用于本规范的术语;译为动词,本规范的术语定义如下。

2.7　Transformation of Predicative to Predicate

当形容词表语和短语表语具有一定的动作意义时,翻译时常将该表语译成谓语。The formula for kinetic energy is applicable to any object that is moving. 将句子中具有动作意义的表语 applicable to 译成动词,做谓语。动能公式适用于任何运动的物体。The smaller the area occupied by the screen material, the greater the chance of a particle reaching an aperture. 将做表语的形容词 smaller, greater 译成谓语。筛面材料所占据的面积越小,颗粒到达筛孔的概率就越大。In many cases, the results of proximate and ultimate analysis are sufficient to indicate how the coal will behave an industrial use. 将做表语的形容词 sufficient 译成谓语。在很多情况下,元素分析和工业

Chapter 2   Transformation of Sentence Constituents

分析的结果都足以说明煤在工业应用中的性质。At present, some old types of engines are still in use. 句中的表语 still in use 具有强烈的动作意义,将其译为谓语。目前,仍在使用一些旧型发动机。

2.8   Transformation of Attribute to Predicate

1. 在汉语中,形容词可以充当谓语,当英语中的形容词做前置定语,难以将它译成通顺的汉语时,可把这一前置形容词定语译成谓语

例如:The highest rate of recovery was at 110 ℃, whereas the lowest rate was at 50 ℃. 将做定语的形容词 highest 和 lowest 译成谓语。回收率在 110 ℃时最高,在 50 ℃时最低。One feature of operation was the very rapid response of furnace to changes in blast temperature and humidity. 将做定语的形容词 rapid 译成谓语。操作的一个特点就是炉子对风温和风湿的变化反应快。Due to the greater open area of coarse screens, the capacity is greater than that of finer screens and in general, the maximum permissible rate of feeding is roughly proportional to the diameter of the apertures. 由于粗孔筛的开孔率较大,因此它比细孔筛的处理量大,一般来说,允许的最大入料量和筛孔的直径大致成正比。

2. 做定语的单词译成谓语

例如:There is a large amount of energy wasted owing to friction. 将句中的定语 wasted 译成谓语。由于摩擦损耗了大量的能量。The initial pilot plant tests produced HWD produces chat had only about 55% solids, much lower than those for the MIRL autoclave tests. 将做定语的介词 produced 译成动词,做谓语。中试厂最初生产的产品固体质量分数只有 55%,远远低于 MIRL 高压釜试验所得到的固体质量分数。

2.9   Transformation of Adverbial to Attribute

有些介词短语形式上是状语,实际上是修饰句中的某个成分,如主语或宾语,这种状语常译成定语。The process cost for this system will dependent on the amount of oil that can be recovered. 这一系统的加工费用取决于能够回收的油量。No data were developed for solvent recovery after drying. 干燥后,没有对溶剂回收的数据进行研究。

In this world, things are complicated and are decided by many factors. 世界上的事情是复杂的,是由各方面的因素决定的。

在这3个句子中,介词短语 for this system, for solvent recovery, in this world 分别修饰主语 the process cost, no data, things,因此这3个介词短语都译成定语。

2.10　Transformation of Subject to Object

1. 被动语态译成主动语态时,将主语译成宾语

例如:The spread of such infectious diseases can be controlled both by proper treatment and disposal of human wastes, and by purification of drinking water supplies. 通过对人类排泄物的适当处理和对饮用水的净化,可以控制这类传染病的传播。Many special precautions must be taken to prevent any kinds of cross-connection between the water system carrying potable water. 为了避免饮用水输送系统之间的交叉接触,必须采取许多特殊的预防措施。

2. 非被动句汉译时,有时也将句子的主语译成宾语

例如:In a absorption system the refrigerant is usually ammonia. 在吸收系统中,通常用氨做冷却剂(表语做主语)。There are many different aspects of communication, first there was the matter of distance. 通信涉及许多方面的问题,首先是距离问题(定语做主语)。Intensive work is now going on to find out even more powerful methods which do not rely on rare U. 目前,正在大力开展科学研究,试图创造出更好的、不依赖铀这种稀有元素的方法。

2.11　Transformation of Attribute to Adverbial

1. 当名词译成动词时,原来修饰该名词的形容词译成副词,做状语

例如:Let's have a good look at page 6. 仔细看一下第6页。To increase precision, the machine tool must also provide rigid control of relative movement between the tool and work. 为了提高精度,机床还应严格地控制刀具与工件之间的相对运动。

Chapter 2 Transformation of Sentence Constituents

2. 当介词短语做定语时,往往可将其转译为汉语句中的状语

例如:The range of concentration of pollutants in the atmosphere is roughly 4 to 5 orders of magnitude. 在大气层中,污染物的浓度范围大约在 4~5 个数量级。

2.12　Transformation of Adverbial to Complement

翻译时常将状语译成汉语的补语。例如:Plastic parts are far lighter than iron ones. 塑料零件比铁轻得多。The particles move faster in the places where the body is being heated. 物体受热的地方,粒子运动得较快。

Chapter 3　　Adjustment of Word and Sentence Order

英语的语言表达方式和句子结构都比较灵活,翻译时应根据汉语习惯,对英语的词序和句序进行调整。所谓词序是指句中各个词的排列顺序,词序的调整主要是对主语、宾语、定语和状语的词序进行调整。所谓句序就是在主从复合句中,主句和从句的排列顺序。

3.1　Adjustment of Word Order

3.1.1　Adjustment of word order of subject

无论英语或汉语,其主语的自然词序均为主语位于动词之前,但在某些情况下的被动句、倒装句等汉译时需要对其主语的位置进行调整。

翻译倒装句时,将其词序调整为自然词序。With the velocity of light travel electro-magnetic waves. 译时将句中的主语 electro-magnetic 放于动词 travel 之前。电磁波以光速传播。Only through much practice shall we be able to master a foreign language. 只有通过大量实践,我们才能掌握一门外语。

被动语态译为主动语态时,将主语译成宾语。Even when the pressure stays the same, great changes in density are caused by changes in temperature. 即使压力保持不变,温度的变化也会引起空气密度的巨大变化。Recently, some new kinds of aeration pipe have been developed in our research institute. 最近,我们研究所研制出了一些新型曝气管。

it 在句中做形式主语或引导强调句型,翻译时常将 it 这一主语省略。It is clear that there are many difficulties for our institute to apply for the project of constructing domestic treatment plant. 显然,对我们学院来说,申请建立污水处理厂的项目是很困难的。

当主语的定语较多、较长时,如果将定语全部译成前置定语,会使句子长而啰嗦,这时可把主语和定语分开译。Analyses for the three tests of reverse osmosis to assess the inflow temperature behavior during continuous processing in the waste water plant are presented in Table I. 句中的主语 analyses 带有很长的定语,由 for the three

Chapter 3 Adjustment of Word and Sentence Order

到 pilot plant 可分开译。表 1 中给出了废水处理厂 3 次连续反渗透实验的分析数据,这些数据用于评价在连续实验过程中,温度对分离性能的影响。

3.1.2 Adjustment of word order of object

宾语的位置一般放在动词之后,但有时也需要把宾语提前。

当宾语带有限定性定语从句时,为了避免译文句子太长,可用介词"对"或"对于"将宾语连同其后的定语从句提到句首。We must carefully process the lean iron ores which are used to produce iron and steel before they are fed to the blast furnace. 将句中的宾语 lean iron ores 连同其后的定语从句提到句首。对于生产钢铁用的贫矿石,我们必须在加入高炉之前仔细加以处理。A special lubrication oil must be used for engines which are operated with fuels, the sulphur content of which is more than 0.5% by weight. 对于所用燃料中硫含量的质量百分比大于 0.5% 的发动机,必须采用专门的润滑油。

当英文句子中有宾语和宾补时,译时常把宾语放在谓语前,而把宾补放在谓语后。We call stored mechanical energy potential energy. 句中宾语 stored mechanical energy 译时提到 call 之前,而宾补 potential energy 仍放于 call 之后。我们把潜在的机械能称为势能。People regard the sun as the chief source of heat and light. 人们把太阳视为主要的热源和光源。We must improve the high temperature strength of this constructional material to a much higher level in order that it can be used to manufacture guided weapons. 我们必须把这种建筑材料的高温强度提得更高,以便能用它来制造导弹。Not only does rolling reduce the metal to the desired thickness, but it toughens the metal. 轧制不仅能将金属减薄到所需要的厚度,也能使金属的韧性增加。

3.1.3 Adjustment of word order of attribute

汉语中的定语一般位于修饰词的前面,按此原则,翻译时将原文中的定语语序进行调整。

1. 单词做定语

单词做前置或后置定语时,翻译时都要前置。例如:a moving body 运动的物体;blue sky 蓝蓝的天;something important 重要的事情。

两个或两个以上的单词共同修饰一个名词做前置定语,翻译时的排列顺序为由后向前译。例如:practical social activities 社会实践活动;theoretical maximum density 最大理论密度；the growing world and home market need 国内外市场日益增长的需要；automatic thermal regulation 温度自动调节器。

但当第一个定语是指示代词或数量形容词时，就需要由前向后译。例如：many developing nations 很多发展中国家；this new aeration cyclone 这台新充气旋流器。

既有前置定语又有后置定语时，需先译后置定语，再译前置定语。例如：many positive features of ED 电渗析的许多优点；this characteristic of magnetic 磁铁的这一性质。

但当前置定语为名词所有格时，却要先译前置定语，再译后置定语。例如：the only source of low cost energy 唯一的廉价能源来源；the theoretical amount of evaporation 理论蒸发量。

2. 短语做定语

介词短语、不定式短语、形容词短语以及分词短语做定语，翻译时都要前置。例如：the wastewater to be treatment 需要处理的废水；the sample being tested 正在测试的样品；substance essential to our life 我们生活中不可缺少的一种物质；an ideal machine for mathematicians to do complicated problems with 数学家用来解决各种难题的理想机器。

两个短语定语共同修饰一个词，翻译时，先译较近的，再译较远的。例如：the influence of temperature on the conductivity of metals 温度对金属导电性的影响；the attraction of the earth for other bodies 地球对其他物体的引力；the ability of metal to be drawn into wire 金属被拉成丝的能力。

几个介词短语构成定语共同修饰一个名词，如果各短语又作为定语，各自修饰它前面的名词，应由远及近翻译。例如：the speed of motion of an object 物体的运动速度。A change in size or temperature of matter 物体体积或温度的变化；the mode of distribution of the mineral species in coals 煤中矿物种类的分布形式。

名词既有前置定语，又有后置定语时，一般要先译后置定语，再译前置定语。例如：row material prices for ploy-ferric silicate 聚铁硅的原料价格；one half of the estimated fresh-water resources in the world. 世界预计淡水资源的一半；the most extensively used indicator on weather radar 气象雷达最常用的显示器；the milk particles thus sprayed are evaporated into milk powder by heated air forced to the chamber. 把雾化好的奶颗粒通过压进干燥室的热空气干燥成奶粉。

3.1.4 Adjustment of word order of adverbial

1. 副词做状语时的位置

英语中的副词修饰形容词、代词、数词、连词、介词短语或另一个副词，通常放于所修

Chapter 3 Adjustment of Word and Sentence Order

饰词的前面,翻译时词序不变。例如:not all substance,修饰代词 all,并非所有的物质;move about extremely fast,修饰副词 fast,运动得非常快;mainly because,修饰连词 because,主要因为;about three-fourths of raw-oil,修饰数词 three-fourths,大约四分之三的原油。

副词修饰动词时,翻译时一般放于动词之前,但有时也放于动词之后,尤其是副词的比较级或最高级做状语时,多在动词后加"得""很"等词。例如:developed rapidly 发展得很快;operate automatically 自动操作。In a solid the molecules move very slowly; in a liquid, they move about more freely; in a gas, they fly about with great speed. 固体中的分子运动得很慢,液体中的分子运动得比较自由,而气体中的分子则以很快的速度到处乱飞。

频度副词及不确定时间的副词,如 usually, generally, constantly 等,翻译时通常放于主要动词之前。例如:Because the induced EMF always act to oppose changes in the original EMF, the former is often referred to counter EMF. 句中副词 always 和 often 分别修饰动词 acts 和 referred。由于感应电动势始终起着反对原电动势变化的作用,所以通常把它称作反电动势。

2. 短语状语的位置

英语中介词短语、分词短语及不定式短语等表示的状语可以放于被修饰词之前或之后,翻译时根据具体情况及汉语表达习惯而定。例如:Nowadays power call be transmitted through long distance. 介词短语 through long distance 做方式状语,修饰动词 transmitted,因此译时把它放于 transmitted 之前。现在,电力能够通过远距离输送。Using radar, one can see the things beyond the visibility of them. 介词短语 using radar 相当于一个条件状语从句,因此翻译时把它放于句首。如果使用雷达,人们就能看到视线以外的东西。Many elements combine with hydrogen to form combustible liquid. 不定式短语 to form combustible liquid 做结果状语,因此,翻译时将它放于最后。许多元素与氢化合,就生成可燃性液体。

3. 一个句子中几个状语同时出现

两个或两个以上的时间状语,翻译时大时间在前,小时间在后。例如:He came back at ten o'clock last night. 他昨天晚上十点钟才回来。

两个或两个以上的地点状语,翻译时大地点在前,小地点在后。例如:Our university is located in Harbin Heilongjiang province. 我们学院位于黑龙江省哈尔滨市。

时间状语和地点状语同时出现,先翻译时间状语,再翻译地点状语。例如:The meeting was held in our workshop yesterday afternoon. 会议是昨天下午在我们车间召开的。

句中各种状语都有时,按照"时间 + 地点 + 其他状语 + 动词"的顺序进行翻译。例如:Many metallic compounds are too used extensively in our everyday life. 句中 in our everyday life 可看成是地点状语,而 extensively 是方式状语。许多金属化合物在日常生活中也广泛地使用着。Very wonderful changes in matter take place before our eyes everyday. before our eyes 可看成是一个地点状语,everyday 为时间状语。物质中很多奇妙的变化每天都在我们眼前发生。

3.2 Adjustment of Sentence Order

句序是指复合句中主句和从句的排列顺序。英、汉两种语言主从句的关系从根本上都可以归纳为时间关系和逻辑关系。句序的处理就是按照汉语的表达习惯,将主句和从句的顺序调整为按时间关系和逻辑关系叙述的顺序。

3.2.1 Time order in complex sentences

英语中表示时间的从句可放在主句之前,也可以放在主句之后。汉语的表达顺序则是按照时间发生的先后顺序进行叙述。因此在翻译时,应按照时间发生的先后顺序进行翻译。

例如:In this process, LRC is dried by contacting the hot recycle hydrogen donor solvent prior to entering the high pressure hydrogen reactor. 这个句子中有两个动作:entering the high pressure hydrogen reactor 和 is dried,其中 entering the high pressure hydrogen reactor 的动作发生于 is dried 之前,因此翻译时先译。在这一工艺中,LRC 进入高压反应器之前,首先和热循环供氢溶剂接触而得到干燥。

The stability issues, however, must be solved before bulk dried LRCs can be considered as a marketable commodity. 这个句中也有两个动作:can be considered as a remarkable commodity 和 must be solved,其中 can be considered as a marketable commodity 的动作发生于 must be solved 之前,因此先译。在大量的 LRCs 被认作是一种可买卖的商品之前,必须解决 3 个稳定性的问题。

He had just flown in the day before from Beijing where he had spent his vacation after the completion of the construction job he had been engaged in the south. 在这个句子中,有 4 个动作。He had just flown in the day before from Beijing. 昨天他刚坐飞机从北京回来。He had spent his vocation in Beijing. 他在北京度假。He had completed his construction job. 他完成了他的建筑工作。He had been engaged in construc-

Chapter 3 Adjustment of Word and Sentence Order

tion job in the south. 他曾在南方从事建筑工作。整句翻译为:他原在南方从事建筑工作,工作完成以后,他到北京度假,昨天坐飞机才回来。

3.2.2 Logical order in complex sentences

英语中表示逻辑关系的复合句有:表示原因和结果的复合句(原因状语从句),表示条件和结果的复合句(条件状语从句),表示目的和结果的复合句(目的状语从句),表示理由与结果的复合句(结果状语从句)。逻辑顺序的调整就是使这些复合句中的各个从句按照先因后果的顺序进行排列。

1. 表示原因和结果的复合句

Moisture is irreversibly removed from the coal by expansion and expulsion from the micro porous by carbon dioxide, which is liberated during decarbonization. 这个句子中有明显表示因果关系的联词,需要仔细阅读这个句子,才能发现各从句之间的逻辑关系。moisture is irreversibly removed 是结果,expansion and expulsion from the micro porous by carbon dioxide 是发生这个结果的条件,非限定性定语从句 which is liberated during decarbonization 说明 carbon dioxide 的起源,也就是 carbon dioxide 产生的原因。由于 carbon dioxide 的产生,才会出现 expansion and expulsion carbon dioxide,从而使 moisture is from the coal。因此翻译时,应先翻译这个非限定定语从句,再翻译 expansion and expulsion dioxide 这个原因,最后译 moisture is from the coal 这个最终结果。整句翻译为:干燥过程中发生了脱基作用,脱除的二氧化碳从煤的毛细孔中排出,从而永久地去除了煤中的内在水分。

Since the inherent strength of LRCs is significantly reduced when it's gel-like structure is destroyed through drying, dried LRCs break down rapidly and generated large amount of fines becoming more susceptible to spontaneous combustion. 这个句子可以分成4个分句:Since the inherent strength of LRCs is significantly reduced; when it's gel-like structure is destroyed through drying; dried LRCs break down rapidly and generated: large amounts of fines; becoming more susceptible to spontaneous combustion. 整句翻译为:通过干燥破坏了 LRCs 的胶体结构,使 LRCs 的内部压强度大大降低,因此,干燥后的 LRCs 很快就发生了裂解,产生了大量的细粒,从而使 LRCs 更易自燃。

2. 表示条件和结果的复合句

在英语的条件状语从句中,一般是条件在前,结果在后,这和汉语的排列顺序是相同的。例如:Suppose we can't get the necessary equipment. What shell we do? 假如我们得不到必要的设备怎么办？If the medium is a solid in which case the electrons are more tightly packed, the electron flow will be slower. 如果介质是固体，电子则聚集得较紧密，因而电子就流动得缓慢。

3. 表示目的和结果的复合句

在英语的目的状语从句中，目的和动作的位置比较灵活。汉语中，一般是目的在前，行动在后。但有时也为了强调目的，把目的放于行动之后，翻译时可根据具体的句子灵活处理。

例如：He got up early in the morning in order to catch the early bus. 在这个句子中目的 in order to catch the early bus 既可放于动作 got up early 之前，也可以放于动作之后。他一大早就起来了，为的是能赶上早班汽车。或者：为了能赶上早班汽车，他一大早就起来了。

It is necessary first to convert the chemical energy into heat by combustion for the purpose that useful work from the chemical energy stored in fuels might be produced. 阅读这个句子就可以发现，在这个句子中必须将目的 useful work might be produced 放在动作 convert the chemical energy into heat by combustion 之前。为了使储存在燃料中的化学能产生有用功，首先要通过燃烧，将化学能转化成热能。

4. 表示理由和结果的复合句

在英语的结果状语从句中，一般是理由在前，结果在后，这和汉语中的排列顺序是相同的。例如：Atom is so small that we can't see them even with the most powerful microscope. 原子非常小，即使用最强大的显微镜也看不到它们。The temperature in the sun is so high that nothing can exist in solid state. 太阳中的温度太高，没有任何物体能够以固态形式存在。

如果原因状语从句或目的状语从句中有连词 such as, such as to, so as, so as to, so that, such that, enough to, 译成汉语时，为了使译文合乎汉语的表达习惯，常不译这些连词，而在句中加"就、得、便、以、能、使、因而、因此、所以"等词，但有时直接译也可以不加任何词，视具体情况而定。例如：The aeration cyclone must be designed as to bring more air into it naturally by jet scream. 旋风除尘器必须设计得带入更多的空气以产生外涡旋。During combustion, the oxidation takes place rapidly enough to be accompanied by light and heat. 在燃烧过程中，氧化作用发生的非常快并伴随着发光、发热。

Chapter 4　Translation of Passive Voice

　　科技英语的一大特点就是在文中大量地使用被动语态。和英语相比,汉语中虽然也使用被动语态,但远不如英语那样广泛,往往有这样的情况,英语中用被动语态表达的句子,汉语中却用主动语态来表示。例如:给"能"下定义时,英语中用"Energy is defined as the ability to do work"这一被动句来表示,而汉语中却用主动句"能的定义为做功的能力"来表达,因此,在翻译被动语态时,必须摆脱原句的语态限制,凡能译成汉语的主动句的,应尽量译为主动句,不宜译成主动句的才译成被动句。这样,翻译出来的句子才符合汉语的表达习惯。

4.1　Translation to Active Sentence

4.1.1　The subject is translated as subject

　　当句中的主语为无生命的名词,且句中没有由 by 引导的行为主体,句中的主语仍做主语。例如:Air-sampling devices are used to detect and measure smoke, particles and gases. 大气采样器用于监测和测量空气中的烟尘、颗粒物和气溶胶。Simply stated, the environment can be defined as one's surroundings. 简单地说,环境的定义为我们周围的环境。Our culture as well as our aesthetic heritage is also being lost to pollution. 我们的文化遗产和艺术遗产正在遭受污染。Many believe that these changes are caused by acidic deposition traceable to pollutant acid precursors that result from the burning of fossil fuels. 许多人相信是酸沉降导致了这些变化,而这些酸性污染物则是源于化石燃料的燃烧。

4.1.2　The subject is translated as object

　　当被动句中有地点状语或由介词 by, from, at, in 等引导的状语时,将此状语译成主语,原主语译为宾语。例如:The concentration of secondary pollutants will be influenced by the same gross atmospheric features, such as air mass origin and degree of dispersion, as the primary pollutants. 与一次污染物相同,像气团源和分散度等的总大气特性会影响二次污染物的浓度。Living spores of various fungi have been collected by plane above the Caribbean Sea, 800 miles from their nearest source. 在加勒比海上空,距最近的污染源 800 m 的飞机上可检测到不同真菌的活性孢子。In spite of the usually low concentration at the source, marine bacteria have been collected 80 miles inland from the nearest coast. 尽管污染源的浓度通常很低,但在离最近海岸 80 m 的岛上已收集到了海洋细菌。

某些要求宾语或宾补的动词用于被动语态,翻译时需要在其前加"人们、大家、有人"等具有广泛意义的词做主语,把原来的主语译做宾语。例如:He was seen to be working in the workshop. 有人看见他在车间工作。Silver is known to be the best conductor. 我们知道,白银是最好的导体。Rubber is found a good insulating material. 人们发现橡胶是一种良好的绝缘材料。

在上面这 3 个短句中,谓语动词 seen, known 和 found 都既带有宾语 him, silver 和 rubber,又带有宾补 to be working in the workshop, to be the best conductor 和 to be a good insulting material,因此翻译时要增加主语。

4.1.3 Translation to judgement sentence

用"的"结构做表语的判断句可用来翻译某些被动句,用"的"结构做主语的判断句尤其适合于用来翻译倒装语序的被动句。

1. 译成用"的"结构做表语的判断句

Rainbows are formed when sunlight pass through small drops of water in the sky. 彩虹是当光线穿过天空中的小水滴时形成的。These analytical equipment are imported from U.S. 这些分析仪器是从美国进口的。These reports should be fully utilized by us when studying a project, as they are the most authoritative records available. 这些报告是我们在研究项目时应该充分利用的,因为它们是可利用的最有权威的资料。

2. 译成用"的"结构做主语的判断句

Produced by electrons are the x-rays, which allow the doctor to look aside a patient's body. 电子产生的是 X 射线,医生用它做透视。Employed to lift the jacks were three hydraulic pumps. 用来提升千斤顶的是 3 台液压泵。Connected with it is a control rod. 与之相连的是一个操纵杆。

Chapter 4 Translation of Passive Voice

4.1.4 Translation of common passive sentence

有一类以 it 做形式主语的被动句,在译文中常常需要译成主动形式,翻译时有时可不加主语,但有时却要加上不确定的主语,如"有人、大家、人们、我们"等。

第一种情况为不加主语的。例如:It is hoped that 希望;It is reported that 据报道;It is said that 据说;It must be supposed that 据猜测;It must be admitted that 必须承认;It must be pointed out that 必须指出;It will be seen from this that 由此可以看出。

另一种情况为加主语的。例如:It is believed that 有人相信;It is generally considered that 大家认为;It is well-known that 大家知道;It was told that 有人说;It is asserted that 有人主张;It is found that 人们发现;It is stressed that 人们强调;It has been suggested that 有人认为。

4.2 Translation to Passive Sentence

汉语有时也采用被动表达,这一类句子都着重被动的动作,有的说出了动作的主动者,有的则说不出动作的主动者。英语的被动句译成汉语的被动句往往采用"被、给、由、受、为……所"等表示被动的助词或字眼。

例如:The sewage of nearly 10 million people in the U.S is discharged raw into our waterways. 近一百万人口的生活污水未经处理直接被排入我们的水道。When these compounds decomposed by bacteria, oxygen is removed from water. 当这些组分由微生物降解时,氧就被从水中排除。It has been suggested that plants be used as indicators of harmful contaminants because of their greater sensitivity to certain specific contaminants. 有人认为植物可被用作有害污染物的指示剂,因为它们对某些特定的污染物非常敏感。In this study, those remaining effects are treated as stochastic noise and are assumed white Gaussian distributed with zero mean. 在这项研究中,那些未被考虑的各影响因素被作为随时噪声加以处理,并假设其具有零均值白高斯分布。The hypothesis has been proved up to the hilt by the results of experiments. 这一假设已为实验结果所证实。

4.3 Translation to Sentence with No Subject

由于内容的缘故,科技文章在讲述什么事情时,常强调怎么做而不介意谁去做,这样许多被动句可译成无主语句,翻译时原被动句中的主语就成了无主语句的宾语。有时,还可以在原主语之前加"把、将、使、对、由"等。

例如:In the opinion of noted economists, three pointed should be kept in mind in maintaining Beijing as the nation's culture and economic center. 著名经济学家认为,北京要继续成为全国的文化和经济中心必须注意3点。Many strange new means of transport have been developed in our century, the strangest of them being perhaps the hovercraft. 在我们这个世纪里研制了许多新颖的交通工具,其中,最奇特的也许就是气垫船了。After reducing the BOD to nominally 60, wastewater treated can be directly discharged into nature water body. 将废水中的BOD降到60以后,处理后的水可直接排入天然水体。

Solid particles must be removed from gaseous effluents because, if they are not removed, they settle out on land and houses, or in people's lungs. 必须将固体颗粒从气态排放物中去除,否则它们会沉降在土壤、房屋上,或沉积在人的胃里。The solids wastes found in the petrochemical industry may be stored, handled, and disposed of by various combinations of many different methods. 可对石油化学工业产生的固体废物进行储存、处理,并可采用不同的方法、通过不同的结合方式进行处置。Usually, before the municipal solid waste can be landfilled, it dose require digestion to avoid odors, insects, and water pollution. 通常在把城市固体废物进行卫生填埋之前,必须进行消化处理,以防散发臭味、滋生细菌、污染水体。

Chapter 5　Translation of Attributive Clause

从和主句关系的密切程度来说,定语从句可分为限定性定语从句和非限定性定语从句。限定性定语从句和主句的关系比较密切,而非限定性定语从句和主句的关系却较为松散。正是由于在文中广泛地使用定语从句,才使得科技文章的句子结构和句子之间的逻辑关系比较复杂。

5.1　Translation of Restrictive Clause

5.1.1　Preposition translation

当定语从句不太长或不太复杂时,可将其译成一个"的"字结构放在被修饰词的前面。

例如:It is the function of the medium recovery system to recovery the magnetite that is rinsed from the products on the rinse screen and to remove the nonmagnetic materials from a portion of the main medium circulation system for viscosity control. 句中 function of the medium recovery system 的主语由两部分组成:to recovery the magnetite and to remove the nonmagnetic materials。因此可将这个长句分成两个分句:to recovery the magnetite that is rinsed from the products on the rinse screen 和 to remove the nonmagnetic materials from a portion of the main medium circulation system for viscosity control。在第一个分句中 that is rinsed from the products on the rinse screen 是定语从句,修饰 magnetite;在第二个分句中 for viscosity control 做目的状语。整句翻译为:介质回收系统的作用是回收经喷淋脱介筛上冲下的磁铁矿和除去部分主要介质循环系统中的非磁性物以控制黏度。

The three nutrients that are most needed by plant are nitrogen, phosphorus and potassium. 植物生长所必需的3种营养元素是氮、磷和钾。The other inputs that have been required to increase yields, besides better seeds and large amount of fertilizer, are irrigation systems, pesticides and farm machinery. 除优良的种子和大量的化肥外,要增加产量还必须投入灌溉系统、杀虫剂和农用机械。The earth could be cooled, conceivably to the point of initiating another ice age, if atmospheric contaminants sufficiently reduce the amount of solar energy that penetrate the earth's atmosphere. 如果大气中的污染物能够有效地减少穿过大气层的太阳能,地球将被冷却,到一定程度也许会出现另一个冰河时代。X-rays structure analysis can be used particularly in the investigation of two-phase alloys where the crystal type can be determined only crystal graphically. X 射线结构分析法尤其适用于研究那些只能从结晶学上确定其晶体类型的二相合金。We are a long way to go from a technology that will restore the particulate matter level of the atmosphere to that of a century or more ago. 要发明一项使大气中颗粒物恢复到约一个世纪以前的水平的技术,我们还需经过长期的努力。

5.1.2　Split translation

把定语从句译成主句的并列句,放于主句之后,分译法适用于以下两种情况:限定性定语从句较长或限定性定语从句虽不太长、但先行词的修饰成分较多,如果采用前置法,将定语从句放于被修饰词之前,就会使译文层次模糊、表达不清。

分译法有两种形式,重复先行词和省略先行词。重复先行词的词义可用"他、它、他们、它们"或"这些、那些"等代词来代表先行词的词义。

例如:Corrosion is an electro-chemical process by which a metal, such as, mild steel, returns to its natural state, such as iron oxide or rust. 句中由 which 引导的定语从句修饰 process,而 process 还有前置定语 an electro-chemical,并且从句在语义上是为了进一步说明,故为了使译文层次分明、表达清晰,采用分译法,并重复先行词。整句翻译为:腐蚀是一种电化学过程,在这一过程中像低碳钢之类的金属会恢复到其自然状态,如铁以氧化铁或铁锈状态存在。

There is an ozone layer in the lower stratosphere that absorbs an appreciable part of the energy in the ultraviolet wavelengths emitted by the sun. 臭氧层存在于低层平流层中,它能吸收太阳辐射的紫外长波的部分能量。Dust and other particles matter in the air provide nuclei around which condensation takes place, forming droplet and thereby playing a role in snowfall and rainfall patterns. 尘粒和空气中的其他颗粒物提供了周围能发生浓集作用的核,进而形成微滴,在降雨或降雪中起到一定的作用。

The contaminants whose buildup in the atmosphere could hypothetically cause reduced penetration of solar energy are suspended particulates that have the ability to absorb and scatter solar energy. 句中有两个定语从句,分别为修饰 contaminants 的从句 whose buildup in...penetration of solar energy 和修饰 suspended particulates 的从句 that have the ability solar energy。翻译时考虑到译文结构紧凑,逻辑性强,第一个从句采用前置法,而第二个则采用分译法。整句翻译为:堆积在大气层中,假定能减少

太阳能透射的污染物的是一些悬浮颗粒,这些颗粒能吸收和分散太阳能。

The gases pollutants are usually formed in homogeneous gas-phase reactions which in many cases are photochemical initiated. 句中 which 引导的定语从句虽不长,但其先行词 reactions 的修饰成分比较多,需采用分译法,重复先行词。整句翻译为:气态污染物通常是在均质的气相反应中形成的,多数情况下,这些反应都是由光化作用推动的。

有时省略先行词代表的意义也能达到层次分明、语义清楚的目的。例如:The activated silica gel can be composted into flocculants which are being tested in domestic sewage to remove nitrogen and phosphorous. 活化后的水玻璃可制成复合型的絮凝剂,用于生活污水脱氮除磷的试验研究。Figure 1 incorporates many of the factors which must be considered in developing a satisfactory system. 图 1 所示的许多因素,在研制性能良好的系统时必须予以考虑。The energy obtained from uranium atoms in nuclear-power stations may be used to heat boilers and produce steam for the turbines that derive the alternators. 从原子能发电厂中的铀元素中获得的能量可以用来加热锅炉,产生蒸汽、驱动气轮机,以带动交流发电机。

Devolatilized tar, being hydrophobic, remains on the coal surface in the pressured aqueous environment, producing a uniform coating that seals the micro porous limits moisture reapportion. 这个句子的逻辑关系比较复杂:being hydrophobic 可以有两种理解,对主语 devolatilized tar 进行补充说明或作为 remains on the coal surface 的原因。分词短语 producing a uniform coating 是 remains on the coal surface 的结果。seals the micro porous limits moisture reapportion 是 producing a uniform coating 的结果。连词 and 连接的两个动词 seals 和 limits 之间也有逻辑关系。limits moisture reapportion 是 seals the micro porous 的结果。

在一般句子中,要补译出表示句子之间逻辑关系的关联词,但此句的逻辑关系比较复杂,如果将这些关联词补译出来,会使句子显得十分啰嗦,试比较如下。

加关联词译:经脱挥发作用得到的焦油由于是疏水的,因此在高压的液相中仍然留在煤的表面,从而形成一层均匀的油膜,从而封住了煤中的微孔,所以减少了煤对水分的重新吸附。

不加关联词译:经脱挥发作用得到的焦油是疏水的,在高压的液相中仍然留在煤的表面,形成一层均匀的油膜,封住了煤中的微孔,从而减少了煤对水分的重新吸附。

5.1.3　Integration translation

把原句中的主语和定语从句融合在一起,用原句的主语做主语部分,原句中的定语从句做谓语部分,译成一个独立句子。

1. There be 结构中的定语从句在翻译时常采用融合法

There are some metals which are lighter than water. 有些金属比水轻。There are many new technologies and devices which are used to remove the nitrogen and phosphorous in wastewater. 此句中将 There be 句中的 many new technologies and devices 译成句子的主语,定语从句中除 which 以外的部分做句子的谓语,同时将它译成被动语态。很多新技术和新设备被用于去除废水中的氮和磷。There are many diseases which are associated with the contamination of water supplies by animal or human wastes. 很多种疾病与因人畜排泄物所引起的供水污染有关。

2. 除了 There be 结构中的定语从句外,其他一些定语从句也可采用融合法进行翻译

The chemical properties of a certain element which depend on the arrangement of these electrons, particular the outer, or valence electrons, are the same. 如果将 which 引导的定语从句译成主句的并列句,会使句子的意思显得松散,不连贯,试比较如下。

分译:各元素的化学性质是一样的,这一性质取决于电子(尤其是外层电子)的排列方式。

合译:元素的化学性质取决于电子(尤其是外层电子)的排列方式,在这一点上各元素是一样的。

Low mining cost, high reactivity and extremely low sulphur content make these coals premium fuels if not for their high moisture levels which range from 25% to more than 60%. 试对分译与合译进行如下比较。

分译:低开采成本、高反应活性以及很低的硫分会使这些 LRCs 成为优质燃料,如果不是由于它们的水分含量很高的话,这些煤的水分含量达 25%~60%。

合译:如果不是由于它们的水分含量高达 25%~60% 的话,低开采成本、高反应活性以及很低的硫分会使这些 LRCs 成为优质燃料。

Besides carbon dioxide, scientists identify other gases that are thought to contribute to global warming. 除了二氧化碳外,科学家已证实还有其他一些气体也在促使全球变暖。

5.2 Translation of Non-restrictive Clause

非限定性定语从句对先行词不起限制作用,只对它加以描述、叙述或解释,翻译时可采用下列几种方法。

5.2.1　Preposition translation

对于较短而具有描写性的非限定性定语从句,也可译成带"的"字结构的前置定语。

Alkali cation, a major source of boiler fouling, which is associated with the carboxyl group, are released in the aqueous phase and can be removed during the final mechanical dewatering. 将 which 引导的非限定性定语从句译成前置定语,同时将 associated with 引申为"结合、化合"。将做主语补足语的 a major source of boiler fouling 译成表语。整句翻译为:与羟基相结合的碱离子是锅炉堵塞物的主要来源,它们在干燥过程中被释放到液相中,在最后的机械脱水阶段被去除。

Hydrogen, which is lightest element, has only one electron. 元素中最轻的氢元素只有一个电子。

The mercury, which is biologically concentrated as it passes along the food chain, was contaminating the fish which were being consumed by the local residents, leading to the poisonings. 句中的非限定性定语从句 which is biologically concentrated as it passes along the food chain 是对先行词 mercury 的进一步描述,翻译时采用前置法,而句中的限定性定语从句 which were being consumed by the local residents 则采用分译法为好。整句翻译为:通过食物链的生物作用富集的汞会污染鱼类,当地的居民食用了受污染的鱼会导致中毒。

5.2.2　Split translation

采用分割法在引导词前切断,将从句译成汉语中联合复句中的分句。

1. 重复先行词所代表的含义

Conditions are created in agriculture that favors the crop pest, which upsets the balance between it and its natural enemies so that some kind of external control is necessary. 该句子结构比较复杂,condition 带有两个从句,一个由 that 引导的限定性定语从句,一个由 which 引导的非限定性定语从句,句中还有由 so that 引导的目的状语从句。整句翻译为:农业生产为作物病虫的生长创造了条件,这打破了病虫和它的天敌之间的平衡,因此须采取外部措施加以控制。

The problems with the combustion reaction occur because the process also produces many other products, most of which are termed air pollutants. 伴随着燃烧出现了一些问题,因为燃烧过程会产生许多其他的产物,它们多数被称为空气污染物。

Some communities use what are called stabilization or oxidation ponds, which are large ponds about 3 feet deep with a surface area of about 1 acre for every 1 000 people to be served. 一些社区使用所谓的氧化池或稳定池，它们大约3英尺深，为每1 000人提供的服务表面积约为1英亩。

2. 省略先行词所代表的含义

The humus gets mixed with the mineral components of the soil by the burrowing activities of countless soil organisms, which helps to distribute these essential nutrients throughout the soil. 腐殖土利用无数土壤生物体的活性与土壤中的各种矿物组分混合，使其中的基本养分能充分分散到土壤中。

The principal technological changes in the engineering control of air pollution were the perfection of the motor-driven fan, which allowed large scale gas-treating systems to be built; the invention of the electrical precipitator, which made particulate control in many processes feasible. 大气污染控制工程中的主要技术变化是电动通风扇的完善，并因此建成了大型大气处理系统；电除尘器的发明使许多工艺中颗粒物的控制成为可能。

5.2.3　Translation to independent sentence

以which引导的特种定语从句通常是说明整个句子的，是对主句所叙述的事实或现象加以总结、概括、补充说明或承上启下的，翻译时主句和从句分译，通常将which译成"这……"，但有时也可译成"从而……""因而……"。

Many cities add a little chlorine to their water supplies to kill bacteria, which it does most efficiently and cheaply. 许多城市在供水中加入少量的氯杀菌，在这方面氯气既经济又有效。

Recently, hydrocarbons have received considerable attention as air pollutants because they may participate in reaction, in the atmosphere, which produce objectionable intermediate compounds and products. 近来，碳氢化合物作为一种大气污染物得到了很多关注，因为它们在大气中能参与反应，产生有毒、有害的中间化合物和产物。

Some ground waters contain natural concentrations of fluorides, which reduce the incidence of dental cavities in children but which in larger concentrations coastal the teeth. 一些地表水本身含有一定浓度的氟化物，这能减少儿童虫牙的发病率，但浓度过高则会损坏牙齿。

High population density is responsible for much of the destruction of coastal

Chapter 5　Translation of Attributive Clause

habitats, which is a global problem. 高的人口密度对沿海大部分动物栖息地的破坏负有责任,这是一个全球性问题。

5.2.4　Translation to adverbial clause

英语中的有些定语从句兼有状语从句的职能,在意义上和主句有状语关系,说明主句所发生的原因、结果和目的,或对主句所发生的动作进行假设,翻译时应仔细体会主句和定语从句之间的逻辑关系。

1. 译成表示原因的分句

We know that a cat, whose eyes can take in more rays of light than our eyes, can see clearly in the night. 我们知道,由于猫的眼睛比我们的眼睛能吸收更多的光线,因此它在夜间也能看得很清楚。The ambassador was giving a dinner for a few people, whom he wished especially to talk to or to hear from. 大使只宴请了几个人,因为特地想和他们谈谈,听听他们的意见。Einstein, who worked out the famous theory of Relativity, won the Nobel Prize in 1921. 由于爱因斯坦提出了著名的相对论理论,因此他于 1921 年获得了诺贝尔奖。The only obvious exception to this general statement is the type of waste produced in the textile industry, where the production of mixed-fiber materials complicates the reuse and recycling of fiber materials. 对此唯一明显的例外就是在纺织工业中产生的废料,因其产生的混合纤维使得纤维的回收和重新利用复杂化。This "greenhouse effect" is due primarily to water vapor and carbon dioxide, which have strong infrared absorption bands. 这种"温室效应"主要是由于水蒸气和二氧化碳的作用,因为它们有较强的红外吸收键。However, we can consider ozone in the stratosphere as "good" ozone that protects us from ultraviolet radiation, in contrast to "bad" ozone in the troposphere, which can effect human health. 该句中含有两个定语从句,一个由 that 引导的限定性定语从句修饰 ozone,并为"good" ozone 的原因,可采用分译法;而由 which 引导的非限定性定语从句修饰"bad" ozone,译成表示原因的分句。整句翻译为:然而,我们认为等温层中的臭氧是有益的,因为它可以保护我们不受紫外线的伤害;相反,对流层中的臭氧是有害的,它会影响人们的健康。

2. 译成表示结果的分句

When transported, the products from all over drying systems have suffered from instability problems, which result in excessive fines generation and spontaneous heating. 进行运输时,由于这些产品的质量不稳定,从而导致大量的细粒产生和自燃。High vibration rates can, in general, be used with higher feed-rates, as the deeper bed of material has a "cushioning" effect which inhibits particle bounce. 通常在入料量较大的情况下可以使用较高的振动速度,因为较厚的入料层可以起到"软垫"的作用。Global warming may result in increased cloudiness, which would reduce incoming radiation and counteract warming. 全球变暖会导致云量增多,云量增多可以减少入射辐射,阻碍变暖。

3. 译成表示让步的分句

He insisted on building another house, which he had no use for. 尽管并不需要,他还是坚持要建另一座房子。Atoms, which are very small, can be broken up into still smaller particles——electrons, protons and neutrons. 尽管原子非常小,但仍可以被再分成更小的粒子——电子、质子和中子。My assistant, who had carefully read through the instructions before doing his experiment, could not obtain satisfactory results, because he followed them mechanically. 尽管我的助手在实验前仔细阅读了实验指导书,但由于他只是机械照搬,没有得到令人满意的实验结果。The financial savings possible using this technique will also help to minimize any increasing in product costs, which are inevitable in the present circumstances. 采用这种技术可能达到的经济效益,也将有助于最大限度地减小成本的增加,尽管在目前情况下这是不可避免的。

4. 译成表示目的的分句

The characteristic of CWF has contributed to the need for significant expenditure to develop atomizers which will produce droplets ideally only slightly larger than the finely ground coal. 煤水燃料的这种特性是需要大量研制燃烧器的原因之一,产生的液滴在理想的情况下会比磨细的煤粒稍大一点。

Part 2 Reading

Chapter 6 The Environment and Environmental Issues

6.1 What is "The Environment"

Most people care about the environment. But what exactly dose that mean? When we talk about "environment problems" that need to be addressed, what do we have in mind?

The "environment" can mean different things to different people. Simply said, the environment can be defined as one's surroundings. In terms of the environmental engineer's involvement, however, a more specific definition is needed. The unabridged Random House dictionary defines environment as "the aggregate of surrounding things, conditions or influences, especially as affecting the existence or development of someone or something".

Generally, the term environment refers to the physical environment that surrounds us. This includes the air we breathe, the water we drink, and the lands, oceans, rivers, and forests that cover the earth. To an increasing extent it also includes the buildings, highways, and modern infrastructure of urban settings in which a growing proportion of the world's population resides. This environment will directly and indirectly affects the viability of all living things on the planet such as the people, plants, birds, fish, and others animals that we care about.

To the environmental engineer, the word environment may take on global dimensions, may refer to a very localized area in which a specific problem must be addressed, or may, in the case of contained environments, refer to a small volume of liquid, gaseous, or solid materials within a treatment plant reactor.

The global environment consists of the atmosphere, the hydrosphere and the lithosphere in which the life-sustaining resources of the earth are contained. The atmosphere, a mixture of gases extending outward from the surface of the earth, evolved from elements of the earth that were gasified during its formation and metamorphosis. The hydrosphere consists of the oceans, the lakes and streams and the shallow groundwater bodies that interflow with the surface water. The lithosphere is the soil mantle that wraps the core of the earth.

The biosphere, a thin shell that encapsulates the earth, is made up of the atmosphere and lithosphere adjacent to the surface of the earth, together with the hydrosphere. It is within the biosphere that the life forms of earth, including humans, live. Life-sustaining materials in gaseous, liquid, and solid forms are cycled through the biosphere, providing sustenance to all living organisms.

Life-sustaining resources—air, food, and water are withdrawn from the biosphere. It is also into the biosphere that waste products in gaseous, liquid and solid forms are discharged. From the beginning of time, the biosphere has received and assimilated the wastes generated by plant and animal life. Natural systems have been ever active, dispersing smoke from forest fires, diluting animal wastes washed into streams and rivers, and converting debris of past generations of plant and animal life into soil rich enough to support future populations.

For every nature act of pollution, for every undesirable alteration in the physical, chemical, or biological characteristics of the environment, for every incident that eroded the quality of the immediate, or local environment, there were natural actions that restored that quality. Only in recent years has it become apparent that the sustaining and assimilative capacity of the biosphere, though tremendous, is not, after all, infinite. Though the system has operated for millions of years, it has begun to show signs of stress, primarily because of the impact of humans upon the environment.

As we all know that the environment has been changing since time began. Expansion of the scale of human activity in recent years has put so much strain on the natural environment of this planet that in some cases nature can no longer recover. Exceeding the limits of nature's ability to recuperate means that damage or harmful effects in one part of the world do not stop in that area, but go beyond national borders and become environmental problems on a global scale.

As the above definition implies, humans interact with their environment sometimes adversely impacting the environment and sometimes being adversely impacted by pollutants in the environment. An understanding of the nature of the environment and of human interaction with it is a necessary prerequisite to understanding the work of the environmental engineer.

Chapter 6 The Environment and Environmental Issues

6.2 Global Environmental Issues

Global environmental issues are environmental problems with which the damage and effects do not stop at a single country or region, but spread out onto a global scale. Global environmental issues are environmental problems mainly centered in economically developing countries, but requiring international effort from everyone, including economically advanced countries.

6.2.1 Global warming

Global warming is a process in which the surface temperature of the earth rises because of the "greenhouse effect". The greenhouse effect is caused by an increase in greenhouse gasses (carbon dioxide, methane, chlorofluorocarbons, etc.), which we produce as we go about our daily life. The results of global warming are predicted to be higher sea levels, as the seawater expands from the heat, and harsh climatic changes. These changes are expected to exert a big effect on agriculture and ecosystems.

6.2.2 Ozone layer depletion

Ozone is a natural gas that exists in large quantities in the stratosphere, which is one of the upper layers of the Earth's atmosphere. There, ozone works to protect life on earth by absorbing ultraviolet rays and other harmful rays from the sun. This ozone layer is steadily being destroyed by chlorofluorocarbons, halogens and other ozone-depleting substances in the atmosphere. As the ozone layer is destroyed, more harmful ultraviolet rays reach the Earth's surface. This causes skin cancer, cataracts and other health problems and may exert dangerous effects on plankton, agricultural products and all kinds of plants and animals.

6.2.3 Acid rain

Since the industrial revolution, we have been using large quantities of oil, coal and other fossil fuels. The combustion (burning) of fossil fuels generates large amounts of sulfur oxides and nitrogen oxides. Acid rain is rain (or mist) that has picked up these oxides, which have been released into the atmosphere, and deposits them on the ground. In Europe and North America, acid rain and acidification of the soil is promoting the disappearance of forests and the deterioration of historical ruins and other structures. The acidification of lakes and marshes there is causing the extinction of certain fishes and having other ill effects.

6.2.4　Disappearance of tropical forests

Tropical forests are an important source of lumber. At the same time, tropical forests serve the vital role of being wildlife habitats and of absorbing and storing carbon dioxide, which is the main cause of global warming. It is estimated that about 1,540 hectares of tropical forest disappear each year, because of large-scale, slash-and-burn agricultural practices and logging for commercial purposes. The disappearance of tropical forests is raising concerns about the large-scale extinction of certain species of wild life, the destruction of ecosystems, and effects on global warming.

6.2.5　Dwindling variety of wildlife

There are about 1.75 million species of wild life on this planet that have been verified scientifically. The actual number of species could be 10 million or maybe even more than 100 million! But the destruction of wildlife habitats by human activity and the indiscriminate catching and killing of wildlife is causing a sharp decline in the number of wild plants and animals on this planet. This trend is causing concern regarding the loss of precious gene pools and changes in ecosystems.

6.2.6　Marine pollution

Pollution of the Earth's oceans and seas is getting worse. Pollutants are flushed down rivers and streams, and oil spills into the water when tankers and other ships collide and through offshore drilling and other marine resource development. This pollution exerts harmful effects on fish and birds, and the resultant "red tides" cause problems for fisheries.

6.2.7　Transboundary movements of hazardous waste

Expanded human activity has brought with it an increase in the volume of waste generated. The cost for handling this waste has also skyrocketed. This has led industrialized nations to take some of their waste, including recyclable waste, to developing countries. But this waste also contains toxic substances. When the waste is not properly treated, it pollutes the rivers, groundwater and soil of these economically developing countries and becomes an international problem.

6.2.8 Desertification

Desertification (the changing of productive land into barren land) occurs for various reasons: When regions dry out because of a decrease in rainfall caused by climatic changes; when land is over-cultivated, overgrazed or too many trees are taken for firewood, because of increasing populations in economically developing countries; when land is not given enough time to rest between plantings and becomes barren; and other reasons. Today, desertification affects about one-fourth of the Earth's land surface and about one-sixth of its human population (or 900 million people).

Chapter 7 Environmental Economics

7.1 What is Environmental Economics

Environmental economics is a subfield of economics concerned with environmental issues. Quoting from the National bureau of Economic Research Environmental Economics program, Environmental Economics undertakes theoretical or empirical studies of the economic effects of national or local environmental policies around the world. Particular issues include the costs and benefits of alternative environmental policies to deal with air pollution, water quality, toxic substances, solid waste, and global warming. Environmental economics is distinguished from Ecological economics that emphasizes the economy as a subsystem of the ecosystem with its focus upon preserving natural capital. One survey of German economists found that ecological and environmental economics are different schools of economic thought, with ecological economists emphasizing "strong" sustainability and rejecting the proposition that natural capital can be substituted by human-made capital.

7.2 Concepts

Central to environmental economics is the concept of market failure. Market failure means that markets fail to allocate resources efficiently. As stated by Hanley, Shogren, and White (2007) in their textbook Environmental Economics: "A market failure occurs when the market does not allocate scarce resources to generate the greatest social welfare. A wedge exists between what a private person does given market prices and what society might want him or her to do to protect the environment. Such a wedge implies wastefulness or economic inefficiency; resources can be reallocated to make at least one person better off without making anyone else worse off." Common forms of market failure include externalities, non-excludability and non-rivalry.

Assessing the economic value of the environment is a major topic within the field. Use and indirect use are tangible benefits accruing from natural resources or ecosystem services. Non-use values include existence, option, and bequest values. For example, some people may value the existence of a diverse set of species, regardless of the effect of the loss of a species on ecosystem services. The existence of these species may have an option value, as there may be possibility of using it for some human purpose (certain plants may be researched for drugs). Individuals may value the ability to leave a pristine environment to their children.

Use and indirect use values can often be inferred from revealed behavior, such as the cost of taking recreational trips or using hedonic methods in which values are estimated based on observed prices. Non-use values are usually estimated using stated preference methods such as contingent valuation or choice modeling. Contingent valuation typically takes the form of surveys in which people are asked how much they would pay to observe and recreate in the environment (willingness to pay, WTP) or their willingness to accept (WTA) compensation for the destruction of the environmental good. Hedonic pricing examines the effect the environment has on economic decisions through housing prices, traveling expenses, and payments to visit parks.

7.3 Solutions

7.3.1 Environmental regulations

Under this plan, the economic impact has to be estimated by the regulator. Usually this is done using cost-benefit analysis. There is a growing realization that regulations are not as distinct from economic instruments as is commonly asserted by proponents of environmental economics. Regulations are enforced by fines, which operate as a form of tax if pollution rises above the threshold prescribed. Pollution must be monitored and laws enforced, whether under a pollution tax regime or a regulatory regime.

7.3.2 Quotas on pollution

Often it is advocated that pollution reductions should be achieved by way of tradable emissions permits, which if freely traded may ensure that reductions in pollution are achieved at least cost. In theory, if such tradable quotas are allowed, then a firm would reduce its own pollution load only if doing so would cost less than paying someone else to make the same reduction. In practice, tradable permits approaches have had some success, such as the U.S.'s SO_2 trading program or the EU Emissions Trading Scheme, and interest in its application is spreading to other environmental problems.

7.3.3 Taxes and tariffs on pollution/removal of dirty subsidies

Increasing the costs of polluting will discourage polluting, and will provide a "dynamic incentive", that is, the disincentive continues to operate even as pollution levels fall. A pollution tax that reduces pollution to the socially "optimal" level would be set at such a level that pollution occurs only if the benefits to society exceed the costs. Some advocate a major shift from taxation from income and sales taxes to tax on pollution-the so-called "green tax shift".

7.3.4 Better defined property rights

The Coase Theorem states that assigning property rights will lead to an optimal solution, regardless of who receives them, if transaction costs are trivial and the number of parties negotiating is limited. For example, if people living near a factory had a right to clean air and water, or the factory had the right to pollute, then either the factory could pay those affected by the pollution or the people could pay the factory not to pollute. Or, citizens could take action themselves as they would if other property rights were violated. The U.S. River Keepers Law of the 1880s was an early example, giving citizens downstream the right to end pollution upstream themselves if government itself did not act. Many markets for "pollution rights" have been created in the late twentieth century.

New words

distinguish   *vt.* 区分,辨别   *vi.* 区别,区分

proposition	*n.* 提议,主意　*vt.* 向……提议
tangible	*n.* 有形资产
accrue	*vt.* 获得,积累
bequest	*n.* 遗产,遗赠
pristine	*adj.* 原始的,古时的
hedonic	*adj.* 享乐的,快乐的
contingent	*adj.* 因情况而异,不一定的;偶然发生的
distinct	*adj.* 明显的,独特的,清楚的
assert	*vt.* 维护,坚持,断言,主张
proponent	*n.* 支持者,建议者,提出认证遗嘱者
threshold	*n.* 入口,门槛,开始;极限,临界值
prescribe	*vt.* 规定,开药方
regime	*n.* 政权,政体,社会制度,管理体制
incentive	*n.* 动机,刺激　*adj.* 激励的,刺激的

Chapter 8　Water Pollution

8.1　Water Pollution Problems

Comprising over 70% of the Earth's surface, water is undoubtedly the most precious natural resource that exists on our planet. Without water, life on the earth would be non-existent: It is essential for everything on our planet to grow and prosper. Although we recognize this fact, we disregard it by polluting our rivers, lakes, and oceans. Subsequently, we are slowly but surely harming our planet to the point where organisms are dying at a very alarming rate. In addition to innocent organisms dying off, our drinking water has become greatly affected as is our ability to use water for recreational purposes. In order to combat water pollution, we must understand the problems and become part of the solution.

8.1.1　Causes of pollution

Many causes of pollution including sewage and fertilizers contain nutrients such as nitrates and phosphates. In excess levels, nutrients over stimulate the growth of aquatic plants and algae. Excessive growth of these types of organisms consequently clogs our waterways, use up dissolved oxygen as they decompose, and block light to deeper waters. This, in turn, proves very harmful to aquatic organisms as it affects the respiration ability or fish and other invertebrates that reside in water.

Pollution is also caused when silt and other suspended solids, such as soil, wash off plowed fields, construction and logging sites, urban areas, and eroded river banks when it rains. Under natural conditions, lakes, rivers, and other water bodies undergo. Eutrophication is an aging process that slowly fills in the water body with sediment and organic matter. When these sediments enter various bodies of water, fish respiration becomes impaired, plant productivity and water depth become reduced, and aquatic organisms and their environments become suffocated. Pollution in the form of organic material enters waterways in many different forms as sewage, as leaves and grass clippings, or as runoff from livestock feedlots and pastures. When natural bacteria and protozoan in the water break down this organic material, they begin to use up the oxygen dissolved in the water. Many types of fish and bottom-dwelling animals cannot survive when levels of dissolved oxygen drop below two to five parts per million. When this occurs, it kills aquatic organisms in large numbers which leads to disruptions in the food chain.

8.1.2 Classifying water pollution

The major sources of water pollution can be classified as municipal, industrial, and agricultural. Municipal water pollution consists of waste water from homes and commercial establishments. For many years, the main goal of treating municipal wastewater was simply to reduce its content of suspended solids, oxygen-demanding materials, dissolved inorganic compounds, and harmful bacteria. In recent years, however, more stress has been placed on improving means of disposal of the solid residues from the municipal treatment processes. The basic methods of treating municipal wastewater fall into three stages: Primary treatment, including grit removal, screening, grinding, and sedimentation; secondary treatment, which entails oxidation of dissolved organic matter by means of using biologically active sludge, which is then filtered off; and tertiary treatment, in which advanced biological methods of nitrogen removal and chemical and physical methods such as granular filtration and activated carbon absorption are employed. The handling and disposal of solid residues can account for 25 to 50 percent of the capital and operational costs of a treatment plant.

The characteristics of industrial wastewaters can differ considerably both within and among industries. The impact of industrial discharges depends not only on their collective characteristics, such as biochemical oxygen demand and the amount of suspended solids, but also on their content of specific inorganic and organic substances. Three options are available in controlling industrial wastewater. Control can take place at the point of generation in the plant; wastewater can be pretreated for discharge to municipal treatment sources; or wastewater can be treated completely at the plant and either reused or discharged directly into receiving waters.

8.1.3　Point and nonpoint sources

According to the American College Dictionary, pollution is defined as: "to make foul or unclean dirty". Water pollution occurs when a body of water is adversely affected due to the addition of large amounts of materials to the water. When it is unfit for its intended use, water is considered polluted.

Two types of water pollutants exist: point source and nonpoint source. Point sources of pollution occur when harmful substances are emitted directly into a body of water. The Exxon Valdez oil spill best illustrates point source water pollution. A nonpoint source delivers pollutants indirectly through environmental changes. An example of this type of water pollution is when fertilizer from a field is carried into a stream by rain, in the form of run-off which in turn affects aquatic life. The technology exists for point sources of pollution to be monitored and regulated, although political factors may complicate matters. Nonpoint sources are much more difficult to control. Pollution arising from nonpoint sources accounts for a majority of the contaminants in streams and lakes.

8.2　Sewage Treatment

8.2.1　What is sewage treatment

Sewage treatment is the process of removing contaminants from wastewater and household sewage, including runoff (effluents) from domestic, commercial and institutional. It includes physical, chemical, and biological processes to remove physical, chemical and biological contaminants. Its objective is to produce an environmentally safe fluid waste stream (or treated effluent) and a solid waste (or treated sludge) suitable for disposal or reuse (usually as farm fertilizer). Sewage can be treated close to where it is created, a decentralized system (in septic tanks, biofilters or aerobic treatment systems), or be collected and transported by a network of pipes and pump stations to a municipal treatment plant, a centralized system. Sewage treatment generally involves three stages, called primary, secondary and tertiary treatment.

8.2.2 Pretreatment

Pretreatment removes materials that can be easily collected from the raw sewage before they damage or clog the pumps and sewage lines of primary treatment clarifiers (trash, tree limbs, leaves, branches etc.).

Screening—The influent sewage water passes through a bar screen to remove all large objects like cans, rags, sticks, plastic packets etc. carried in the sewage stream. This is most commonly done with an automated mechanically raked bar screen in modern plants serving large populations; whilst in smaller or less modern plants, a manually cleaned screen may be used.

Grit removal—Pretreatment may include a sand or grit channel or chamber, where the velocity of the incoming sewage is adjusted to allow the settlement of sand, grit, stones, and broken glass. These particles may damage pumps and other equipment. For small sanitary sewer systems, the grit chambers may not be necessary, but grit removal is desirable at larger plants.

Flow equalization—Clarifiers and mechanized secondary treatment are more efficient under uniform flow conditions. Equalization basins may be used for temporary storage of diurnal or wet-weather flow peaks. Basins provide a place to temporarily hold incoming sewage during plant maintenance and a means of diluting and distributing batch discharges of toxic or high-strength waste which might otherwise inhibit biological secondary treatment.

Fat and grease removal—In some larger plants, fat and grease are removed by passing the sewage through a small tank where skimmers collect the fat floating on the surface. Air blowers in the base of the tank may also be used to help recover the fat as froth. Many plants, however, use primary clarifiers with mechanical surface skimmers for fat and grease removal.

8.2.3 Primary treatment

In the primary sedimentation stage, sewage flows through large tanks, commonly called "pre-settling basins" "primary sedimentation tanks" or "primary clarifiers". The tanks are used to settle sludge while grease and oils rise to the surface and are skimmed off. Primary settling tanks are usually equipped with mechanically driven scrapers that continually drive the collected sludge towards a hopper in the base of the tank where it is pumped to sludge treatment facilities. Grease and oil from the floating material can sometimes be recovered for saponification.

8.2.4 Secondary treatment

Secondary treatment is designed to substantially degrade the biological contents of the sewage which are derived from human waste, food waste, soaps and detergent. The majority of municipal plants treat the settled sewage liquor using aerobic biological processes. The bacteria and protozoa consume biodegradable soluble organic pollutants and bind much of the less soluble fractions into floc. Secondary treatment systems are classified as fixed-film or suspended-growth systems.

Activated sludge—In general, activated sludge plants encompass a variety of mechanisms and processes that use dissolved oxygen to promote the growth of biological floc that substantially removes organic material. The process traps particulate material and can, under ideal conditions, convert ammonia to nitrite and nitrate ultimately to nitrogen gas.

Aerobic granulation—Activated sludge systems can be transformed into aerobic granular sludge systems which enhance the benefits of activated sludge, like increased biomass retention due to high sludge settlability.

Surface—Most biological oxidation processes for treating industrial wastewaters have in common the use of oxygen (or air) and microbial action. Surface-aerated basins achieve 80% to 90% removal of BOD with retention times of 1 to 10 days. The basins may range in depth from 1.5 to 5.0 meters and use motor-driven aerators floating on the surface of the wastewater.

Filter beds (Oxidizing beds)—In older plants and those receiving variable loadings, trickling filter beds are used where the settled sewage liquor is spread onto the surface of a bed made up of coke (carbonized coal), limestone chips or specially fabricated plastic media. Such media must have large surface areas to support the biofilms that form. The liquor, distributed through perforated spray arms, trickled through the bed and is collected in drains at the base. These drains also provide a source of air which percolates up through the bed, keeping it aerobic. Biological films of bacteria, protozoa and fungi form on the media's surfaces and eat or otherwise reduce the organic content.

Constructed wetlands—Constructed wetlands belong to the family of phytorestoration and ecotechnologies; they provide a high degree of biological improvement and depending on design, act as a primary, secondary and sometimes tertiary treatment. They are being increasingly used, although adequate and experienced designs are more fundamental than for other systems and space limitation may impede their use.

Soil bio-technology—A new process called soil bio-technology (SBT) developed has shown tremendous improvements in process efficiency enabling total water reuse. Typically SBT systems can achieve COD levels less than 10 mg/L from sewage input of COD 400 mg/L. Unlike conventional treatment plants, SBT plants produce insignificant amounts of sludge, precluding the need for sludge disposal areas that are required by other technologies.

Biological aerated filters—Biological Aerated (or Anoxic) Filters (BAF) or Biofilters combine filtration with biological carbon reduction, nitrification or denitrification. BAF usually includes a reactor filled with a filter media either in suspension or supported by a gravel layer at the foot of the filter. Carbon reduction and ammonia conversion occurs in aerobic mode and sometime achieved in a single reactor while nitrate conversion occurs in anoxic mode.

Rotating biological contactors—Rotating biological contactors (RBCs) are mechanical secondary treatment systems, which are robust and capable of withstanding surges in organic load. The rotating disks support the growth of bacteria and microorganisms present in the sewage, which break down and stabilize organic pollutants.

Membrane bioreactors—Membrane bioreactors (MBR) combine activated sludge treatment with a membrane liquid – solid separation process. The membrane component uses low pressure microfiltration or ultrafiltration membranes and eliminates the need for clarification and tertiary filtration. One of the key benefits of an MBR system is that it effectively overcomes the limitations associated with poor settling of sludge in conventional activated sludge (CAS) processes.

Secondary sedimentation—The final step in the secondary treatment stage is to settle out the biological floc or filter material through a secondary clarifier and to produce sewage water containing low levels of organic material and suspended matter.

8.2.5 Tertiary treatment

The purpose of tertiary treatment is to provide a final treatment stage to further improve the effluent quality before it is discharged to the receiving environment. More than one tertiary treatment process may be used at any treatment plant.

Filtration—Sand filtration removes much of the residual suspended matter. Filtration over activated carbon, also called carbon adsorption, removes residual toxins.

Lagooning—Lagooning provides settlement and further biological improvement through storage in large man-made ponds or lagoons. These lagoons are highly aerobic and colonization by native macrophytes, especially reeds, is often encouraged. Small filter feeding invertebrates such as Daphnia and species of Rotifera greatly assist in treatment by removing fine particulates.

Nutrient removal—Wastewater may contain high levels of the nutrients nitrogen and phosphorus. Excessive release to the environment can lead to a buildup of nutrients, called eutrophication, which can in turn encourage the overgrowth of weeds, algae, and cyanobacteria (bluegreen algae). This may cause an algal bloom, a rapid growth in the population of algae. The algae numbers are unsustainable and eventually most of them die.

8.2.6 Disinfection

The purpose of disinfection in the treatment of waste water is to substantially reduce the number of microorganisms in the water to be discharged back into the environment for the later use of drinking, bathing, irrigation, etc.. The effectiveness of disinfection depends on the quality of the water being treated (e.g. cloudiness, pH, etc.), the type of disinfection being used, the disinfectant dosage (concentration and time), and other environmental variables.

8.2.7 Odor control

Odors emitted by sewage treatment are typically an indication of an anaerobic or "septic" condition. Early stages of processing will tend to produce foul smelling gases, with hydrogen sulfide being most common in generating complaints. Large process plants in urban areas will often treat the odors with carbon reactors, a contact media with bio-slimes, small does of chlorine, or circulating fluids to biologically capture and metabolize the obnoxious gases. Other methods of odor control exist, including addition of iron salts, hydrogen peroxide, calcium nitrate, etc. to manage hydrogen sulfide levels.

8.2.8 Sludge treatment and disposal

The purpose of digestion is to reduce the amount of organic matter and the number of disease-causing microorganisms present in the solids. Most common treatment options include anaerobic digestion, aerobic digestion, and composting. Incineration is seldom used.

Anaerobic digestion—Anaerobic digestion is a bacterial process occurring in the presence of oxygen. Under aerobic conditions, bacteria rapidly consume organic matter and convert it into carbon dioxide.

Composting—Composting is also an aerobic process that involves mixing the sludge with sources of carbon such as sawdust, straw or wood chips. In the presence of oxygen, bacteria digest both the wastewater solids and the added carbon source and, in doing so, produce a large amount of heat.

Incineration—Incineration of sludge is less common because of air emissions concerns and the supplemental fuel required for burning the low calorific value sludge and vaporizing residual water.

Sludge disposal—When a liquid sludge is produced, further treatment may be required to make it suitable for final disposal. Typically, sludge is thickened (dewatered) to reduce the volumes transported offsite for disposal. There is no process which completely eliminates the need to dispose of biosolids. There is, however an additional step some cities are taking to superheat sludge and convert it into small pelletized granules that are high in nitrogen and other organic materials.

New words

froth	*n.*	泡沫,口沫
saponification	*n.*	皂化
protozoa	*n.*	原生动物
floc	*n.*	絮凝体,絮状物
settlability	*n.*	可沉降性
lagoon	*n.*	咸水湖
coke	*n.*	焦炭
limestone	*n.*	石灰

perforate	vt. 穿孔,穿孔于
percolate	vt. 使渗出,使过滤　n. 渗滤液
ecotechnology	n. 生态技术
anoxic	adj. 缺氧的
colonization	n. 群落化
macrophyte	n. 大型水生植物
invertebrate	n. 无脊椎动物
Daphnia	n. 水蚤
Rotifera	n. 轮虫纲
septic	n. 腐烂物　adj. 腐败的,腐烂的
thermophilic	adj. 适热的
mesophilic	adj. 适温的
calorific	adj. 发热的
pelletize	vt. 使颗粒状

Chapter 9 Microorganisms

9.1 Biological Components of Sewage

Domestic sewage contains countless numbers of living organisms, most of them too small to be visible except when viewed under a microscope, which is why they are called "micro-organisms". Typically, a domestic sewage prior to entering the treatment plant will contain from 100,000 to 1,000,000 micro-organisms per milliliter. These microbes have their origin from two general sources: sanitary wastes and the soil. Both sewages and soils contain large numbers of micro-organisms—especially bacteria. Generally the micro-organisms can be regarded as a natural living part of the organic matter found in sewages and their presence is most important because they serve a primary function in the degradation of wastes in biological sewage treatment. In a sense the successful operation of a biological sewage treatment plant is dependent upon acknowledge of the activities of the micro-organisms especially the bacteria. Efficient treatment then depends on understanding the requirements for optimal growth as well as recognizing unfavorable conditions.

While the majority of the micro-organisms found in sewages are not harmful to man that is non-pathogenic (do not cause disease), some micro-organisms are pathogenic (disease causing) and always are of great concern in sewage treatment. Among the diseases that are associated with sewages are typhoid fever, dysentery, cholera, and hepatitis. The micro-organisms found in sewages are commonly classified by their appearance (morphology). While all micro-organisms found in sewage treatment plants have some role in the decomposition of wastes, probably the three most significant microbial groups in biological treatment are the bacteria, fungi, and protozoa. Bacteria have the primary role of decomposing sewage compounds, forming settleable solids, and at times are the source of operational problems. The general groups called fungi are significant since many operational problems are caused by members of this group. Protozoa are micro-organisms that play a key role as predators and help control the bacterial populations.

Bacteria are living organisms, microscopic in size. They consist of a single cell organism and are capable of growth in suspended masses as in the activated sludge process or attached as in trickling filters. There are many different kinds of bacteria, too numerous to elaborate. The groups best known to those in the sewage field are the fecal coliforms—a group of bacteria commonly associated with human excretions. Bacteria have the ability to reproduce rapidly when in intimate contact with their nutrient material (e. g. wastes) and feed readily by taking in food directly through their cell wall. Bacteria occur in three basic shapes: rods (or bacilli), spheres (or cocci) and spirals. While all of these forms are found in sewages, quite often they are found individually enmeshed or associated in masses, slimes or "flocs" as in the activated sludge process. While bacteria have a principal role in biological treatment, under some conditions certain bacterial forms (e. g. filamentous bacteria) can cause serious operational problems, especially in settling.

9.1.1 Parasitic bacteria

Parasitic bacteria are those which normally live off of another living organism, known as the host, since they require a food supply already prepared for their consumption, and generally do not develop outside the body of the host. The parasitic bacteria are of importance in sewage. They originate in the intestinal tract of human beings and animals and reach the sewage by means of body discharges. Included among the parasitic bacteria are certain specific types which during their growth within the body of the host, produce toxic or poisonous compounds that cause disease in the host. These bacteria are called pathogenic bacteria. They may be present in sewage receiving the body discharges of persons ill with such diseases as typhoid fever, dysentery, cholera, or other intestinal infections.

9.1.2 Saprophytic bacteria

The saprophytic bacteria are those which feed on dead organic matter, thus decomposing organic solids to obtain their needed nourishment, and producing in turn waste substances which consist of both organic and inorganic solids. By this activity they are of utmost importance in sewage treatment methods designed to facilitate or

Chapter 9 Microorganisms

hasten natural decomposition of the organic solids in sewage. Such processes of decomposition will not progress without their activity. In the absence of bacterial life (sterility), decomposition will not take place. There are many species of saprophytic bacteria, each of which plays a specific role in the breakdown of the organic solids of sewage. Each species tends to die away following completion of its part in the process of decomposition.

All of the bacteria, parasitic and saprophytic, require in addition to food, oxygen for respiration. Certain types of them can use only oxygen dissolved in water, termed dissolved oxygen and sometimes called free or molecular oxygen. These organisms are known as aerobic bacteria and the process of degradation of organic solids which they carry out is termed aerobic decomposition, oxidation or decay. This type of decomposition proceeds in the presence of dissolved oxygen without the production of foul odours or unsightly conditions. Other types of bacteria cannot exist in the presence of dissolved oxygen but must obtain the required supply of this element from the oxygen content of organic and some inorganic solids which is made available by their decomposition. Such micro-organisms are termed anaerobic bacteria and the process of degradation of solids which they bring about is called anaerobic decomposition or putrefaction, that is, decomposition in the absence of dissolved oxygen, which results in the production of foul odors and unsightly conditions.

To complicate the reactions involved in the decay of organic matter, certain aerobic types can adjust themselves to live and function in the absence of dissolved oxygen and are termed facultative aerobic bacteria. Conversely, some varieties of anaerobic bacteria can become accustomed to live and grow in the presence of dissolved oxygen and are thus termed facultative anaerobic bacteria.

Such adaptability of the saprophytic bacteria to various sources of oxygen of great importance in the decomposition of organic solids in sewage and thus in the various treatment procedures.

In addition to food and oxygen, bacteria require moisture to remain alive. This is adequately provided in sewage by its water component. In order to function at maximum efficiency bacteria require a favorable temperature. They are very susceptible to changes in temperature in that their rate of growth and reproduction, which is directly proportional to the amount of work done, is definitely and sharply affected by such variations. The larger proportion of the saprophytic types thrive best at temperatures from 20 ℃ to 40 ℃, or 68 ℉ to 104 ℉. These are known as mesophilic types. Variations from this temperature range limit the activity of mesophilic bacteria, practically eliminating it at extremely low temperatures and at high temperatures. Mesophilic sludge digestion proceeds most rapidly at 35 ℃ or 95 ℉. Other bacteria live best at high temperatures, in the range of 55 ℃ to 60 ℃, or 130 ℉ to 140 ℉. These are known as thermophilic types. Thermophilic bacteria function in sewage treatment principally in high temperature digestion of sludge solids. A very few types of bacteria find their optimum conditions at low temperatures, 0 ℃ to 5 ℃, or 32 ℉ to 40 ℉. These are known as psychrophylic bacteria. Temperatures are of major importance in the operation of sewage treatment processes.

When all of these environmental conditions of food supply, oxygen, moisture, and temperature are properly maintained at their optimum amounts for the full functioning of the bacteria, decomposition of the sewage solids proceeds in a natural orderly manner.

Among the other microbiological components that are found in domestic sewages in smaller numbers are viruses. Viruses are very small and can be seen only by use of a sophisticated tool called an electron microscope. Viruses are significant since they all must derive their energy and reproduce from living tissue and are thus parasitic. Among the viruses which are found in domestic sewages which cause diseases in man is hepatitis, polio, as well as a variety of intestinal viruses such as ECHO, coxsackie and adenovirus. A common virus found in domestic sewage that does not infect man but does attack bacteria is a phage or a bacteriophage. Viruses pathogenic to man are usually present in small numbers in relation to coliform bacteria, for example, it is estimated that for approximately every million coliform bacteria there is one infective virus present. Viruses are of special concern in sewage treatment since many are not destroyed by conventional chlorination procedures.

In addition to the groups of microscopic organisms described above, many larger more complex organisms are found in the biological component of sewage and play a part in the decomposition of organic matter. These are termed macroscopic, that is visible to the naked eye. They include varieties of worms and insects in various stages of development. Some are active in sewage treatment plant facilities and others are prevalent in highly polluted streams.

Certain forms of all of these organisms, microscopic and macroscopic, are essential to the orderly decomposition of organic matter in nature, and hence are equally important for the proper functioning of the usual methods of sewage treatment. As noted, it is the biological organisms that actually carry on the processes of biological waste treatment. A prime responsibility of the operator is to provide the environmental condition best suited for their growth.

9.2 Anaerobic Digestion

Anaerobic digestion is a complex biochemical reaction carried out in a number of steps by several types of micro-organisms that require little or no oxygen to live. During the process, a gas principally composed of methane (CH_4) and carbon dioxide (CO_2). Otherwise known as biogas, is produced. The amount of gas produced varies with the amount of organic waste fed to the digester and temperature influences the rate of decomposition (and gas production).

Anaerobic digestion occurs in four distinct steps, illustrated in Figure 9.1.

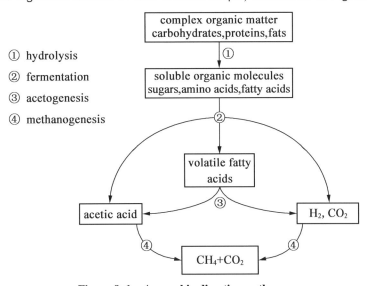

Figure 9.1 Anaerobic digestion pathway

Hydrolysis—Complex organic matter is decomposed into simple soluble organic molecules using water to split the chemical bonds between the substances.

Fermentation or acidogenesis—The chemical decomposition of carbohydrates by enzymes, bacteria, yeasts, or molds in the absence of oxygen.

Acetogenesis—The fermentation products are converted into acetate, hydrogen and carbon dioxide by so-called acetogenic bacteria.

Methanogenesis—Methane (CH_4) is formed from acetate and hydrogen/carbon dioxide by methanogenic bacteria.

The acetogenic bacteria grow in close association with the methanogenic bacteria during the fourth stage of the process. The reason for this is that the conversion of the fermentation products by the acetogens is thermodynamically only possible if the hydrogen concentration is kept sufficiently low. This requires a close symbiotic relationship between both classes of bacteria.

The anaerobic process only takes place under strict anaerobic conditions (i.e. absence of oxygen and very low redox potential). It requires specific adapted biosolids and particular process conditions, which differ considerably from those needed for aerobic treatment.

After completion of the anaerobic digestion steps, the pollutants in the wastewater are transformed into methane (CH_4), carbon dioxide (CO_2) and a small amount of biosolids. Since the solubility of methane in water is very low, it escapes as methane gas.

As a result, a significant part of the energy originating from the pollutants leaves the system as biogas, leaving only a fraction of the initial energy for assimilation by the biomass. Hence the amount of energy generated, by this pathway, which can be used by the biomass is only a small fraction of the total energy content of the incoming pollutants. Biomass growth is therefore much lower compared to the one prevailing in the aerobic processes. For that reason, anaerobic treatment produces between five and ten times less biosolids (sludge) than aerobic processes.

In addition, anaerobic biosolids have the advantage of being much more compact than aerobic biosolids. The dry solids content of anaerobic biosolids range from 2% (for a digestor) to more than 8% for an upflow anaerobic biosolids blanket process. Furthermore, anaerobic biosolids have much better dewatering characteristics compared to aerobic biosolids; as a result, the volume of dewatered biosolids coming from an anaerobic treatment is 7 to 12 times lower compared to aerobic processes.

Another advantage is that anaerobic digestion does not require energy-consuming aeration equipment. The production of biogas during the process even results in a positive energy balance. For this reason the Biotank is designed to first process the effluent using anaerobic digestion and then aerobic digestion

However, anaerobic digestion has its drawbacks. The main one is that it requires more stringent process control and only reduces the organic pollution by 85% to 90%, which means a second step is usually needed to guarantee high effluent quality. This is usually an aerobic stage for polishing before discharge.

As anaerobic biosolids production is rather low, the nutrient removal (nitrogen and phosphorus) is equally low as well. This is one more reason for applying an aerobic second stage, which removes the residual nutrients which would otherwise cause eutrophication of the river in which the treated effluent is discharged.

New Words

acetate	n.	[化学]醋酸盐,醋酸酯
assimilation	n.	吸收(作用),同化作用
biotank	n.	生物反应器
bond	n.	键
digestion	n.	消化,消化作用
enzyme	n.	酶
genesis	n.	成因,起因,生产,发生
fermentation	n.	发酵
hydrolysis	n.	水解(作用)

Chapter 10　Air Pollution

10.1　Air Pollution Problems

Air is the ocean we breathe. Air supplies us with oxygen which is essential for our bodies to live. Air is 99.9% nitrogen, oxygen, water vapor and inert gases. Human activities can release substances into the air, some of which can cause problems for humans, plants, and animals.

Air pollution is normally defined as air that contains one or more chemicals in high enough concentrations to harm humans, other animals, vegetation or materials. There are two major types of air pollutants. A primary air pollutant is a chemical added directly to the air that occurs in a harmful concentration. It can be a natural air component, such as carbon dioxide, that rises above its normal concentration, or something not usually found in the air, such as a lead compound emitted by cars burning leaded gasoline. A secondary air pollutant is a harmful chemical formed in the atmosphere through a chemical reaction among air components. Serious air pollution usually results over a city or other area that is emitting high levels of pollutants during a period of air stagnation. The geographic location of some heavily populated cities, such as Los Angeles and Mexico City, makes them particularly susceptible to frequent air stagnation and pollution buildup.

There are several main types of pollution and well-known effects of pollution which are commonly discussed. These include smog, acid rain, the greenhouse effect, and "holes" in the ozone layer. Each of these problems has serious implications for our health and well-being as well as for the whole environment.

One type of air pollution is the release of particles into the air from burning fuel for energy. Diesel smoke is a good example of this particulate matter. The particles are very small pieces of matter measuring about 2.5 microns or about 0.000,1 inches. This type of pollution is sometimes referred to as black carbon pollution. The

Chapter 10 Air Pollution

exhaust from burning fuels in automobiles, homes, and industries is a major source of pollution in the air. Some authorities believe that even the burning of wood and charcoal in fireplaces and barbeques can release significant quantities of soot into the air.

Another type of pollution is the release of noxious gases, such as sulfur dioxide, carbon monoxide, nitrogen oxides, and chemical vapors. These can take part in further chemical reactions once they are in the atmosphere, forming smog and acid rain.

Pollution also needs to be considered inside our homes, offices, and schools. Some of these pollutants can be created by indoor activities such as smoking and cooking. In the United States, people spend about 80% to 90% of our time inside buildings, and so their exposure to harmful indoor pollutants can be serious. It is therefore important to consider both indoor and outdoor air pollution.

10.1.1 Outdoor air pollution

Smog is a type of large-scale outdoor pollution. It is caused by chemical reactions between pollutants derived from different sources, primarily automobile exhaust and industrial emissions. Cities are often centers of these types of activities, and many suffer from the effects of smog, especially during the warm months of the year. For each city, the exact causes of pollution may be different. Depending on the geographical location, temperature, wind and weather factors, pollution is dispersed differently. However, sometimes this does not happen and the pollution can build up to dangerous levels. A temperature inversion occurs when air close to the earth is cooler than the air above it. Under these conditions the pollution cannot rise and be dispersed. Cities surrounded by mountains also experience trapping of pollution. Inversion can happen in any season. Winter inversions are likely to cause particulate and carbon monoxide pollution. Summer inversions are more likely to create smog.

Another consequence of outdoor air pollution is acid rain. When a pollutant, such as sulfuric acid combines with droplets of water in the air, the water (or snow) can become acidified. The effects of acid rain on the environment can be very serious. It damages plants by destroying their leaves, it poisons the soil, and it changes the chemistry of lakes and streams. Damage due to acid rain kills trees and harms animals, fish, and other wildlife. The Environmental Protection Agency (EPA), and Environment Canada are among the organizations that are actively studying the acid rain problem.

The Greenhouse Effect, also referred to as global warming, is generally believed to come from the build up of carbon dioxide gas in the atmosphere. Carbon dioxide is produced when fuels are burned. Plants convert carbon dioxide back to oxygen, but the release of carbon dioxide from human activities is higher than the world's plants can process. The situation is made worse since many of the earth's forests are being removed, and plant life is being damaged by acid rain. Thus, the amount of carbon dioxide in the air is continuing to increase. This buildup acts like a blanket and traps heat close to the surface of our earth. Changes of even a few degrees will affect us all through changes in the climate and even the possibility that the polar ice caps may melt. (One of the consequences of polar ice cap melting would be arising in global sea level, resulting in widespread coastal flooding.)

Ozone depletion is another result of pollution. Chemicals released by our activities affect the stratosphere, one of the atmospheric layers surrounding earth. The ozone layer in the stratosphere protects the earth from harmful ultraviolet radiation from the sun. Release of chlorofluorocarbons (CFC's) from aerosol cans, cooling systems and refrigerator equipment removes some of the ozone, causing "holes"; to open up in this layer and allowing the radiation to reach the earth. Ultraviolet radiation is known to cause skin cancer and has damaging effects on plants and wildlife.

10.1.2 Indoor air pollution

Many people spend large portion of time indoors as much as 80% to 90% of their lives. We work, study, eat, drink and sleep in enclosed environments where air circulation may be restricted. For these reasons, some experts feel that more people suffer from the effects of indoor air pollution than outdoor pollution.

There are many sources of indoor air pollution. Tobacco smoke, cooking and heating appliances, and vapors from building materials, paints, furniture, etc. cause pollution inside buildings. Radon is a natural radioactive gas released from the earth, and it can be found concentrated in basements in some parts of the United States. Pollution exposure at home and work is often greater than outdoors. The California Air Resources Board estimates that indoor air pollutant levels are 25% to 62% greater than outside levels and can pose serious health problems.

Chapter 10　Air Pollution

10.2　Air Pollutants

Air pollutants are termed as materials which are discharged into the atmosphere as a result of human activities. These materials may be classified as two types: one type is called as primary pollutants, which are released directly into air in a harmful form; the other is secondary pollutants, which are modified into a hazardous form after they enter the atmosphere due to chemical reactions or which are formed in the atmosphere.

10.2.1　Primary pollutants

Typical primary pollutants include particulates, sulfur dioxide, carbon oxides, nitrogen compounds and hydrocarbons.

1. Particulates

Particulates are small pieces of solid or liquid materials dispersed in the atmosphere, constitute the third largest category of air pollutant. These include dust, ash, soot, smoke, and droplets of pollutants either emitted to the air or formed in the atmosphere. Particulates are characterized as 0.005 to 100 μm in size. The major human sources of particulates are from unburned fuels from stationary fuel combustion and transportation as well as industrial processes. The impacts of particulates range from reduced visibility and soiling of exposed surfaces to respiratory problems and carcinogenicity. Respirable particles (PM2.5) are especially problematic because they can be drawn deep into the lungs, where they can damage respiratory tissues.

2. Sulfur dioxide (SO_2)

Sulfur dioxide is a colorless corrosive gas that is a respiratory irritant and a poison. It is also of major concern because it can react in the atmosphere with ozone, water vapor, and other materials to form sulfuric acid (H_2SO_4). Sulfuric acid, one of the strongest oxidizing agents known, can cause substantial damage to construction materials, metals, and other materials. It can also form very small aerosols or attach to minute aerosols, which can travel deep into the respiratory system when inhaled, doing serious tissue damage.

The major anthropogenic sources of sulfur dioxide emissions to the atmosphere are combustion of sulfur—containing fuels (coal and oil) and industrial processes. More than 70 percent of the sulfur dioxide in our air in urban areas comes from coal-burning electrical power plants. It has been estimated that a power station burning 5,000 tones of coal per day may discharge 500 tones of sulphur dioxides into the air.

3. Carbon oxides (CO and CO_2)

Carbon monoxide is a colorless, odorless, nonirritating poison that can quickly cause death at quite low concentrations. Inhaled carbon monoxide will tightly attach to hemoglobin in blood, reducing the capacity of the blood to carry oxygen to bodily tissues. The result is headaches, drowsiness, and eventually asphyxiation. Carbon monoxide is produced when organic materials such as gasoline, coal, or wood are incompletely burned. The automobile is responsible for most of the carbon monoxide produced in cities (67 percent), but stationary fuel combustion (20 percent) and industrial processes (6 percent) also contribute.

Carbon dioxides have received considerable attention as air pollutants because the increasing concentrations of carbon dioxide have been implicated in global warming.

4. Nitrogen oxides (NO_x)

Nitrogen oxides are highly reactive gases formed from oxidation of the nitrogen in air during combustion. When combustion takes place in air at a temperature above about 2,000 °F, the nitrogen and oxygen molecules in air may react with each other forming oxides of nitrogen:

$$N_2 + O_2 \rightarrow 2NO \quad \text{(nitrogen oxide)}$$
$$2NO + O_2 \rightarrow 2NO_2 \quad \text{(nitrogen dioxide)}$$

The designation NO_x is often used to signify mixtures of NO and NO_2 in air. The nitrogen dioxide is a critical component in smog-forming reactions. Nitrogen oxides can also react with water vapor, forming nitric acid (HNO_3), and contribute to acid precipitation problems.

The primary source of NO_x is the automobile engine, although combustion of coal, oil, or natural gas at high enough temperatures can also contribute to the problem. Ironically, an excellent way to minimize emissions of hydrocarbons and carbon monoxide is to burn fuels at high temperatures with an abundance of air, but this then increases the amount of NO_x emitted.

5. Hydrocarbons

Hydrocarbons constitute a large group of volatile organic compounds. The major anthropogenic sources of hydrocarbons emitted to the atmosphere are evaporation of petroleum-based fuels and remnants of the fuels that did not burn completely.

Local high concentrations of hydrocarbons in the air are common in garages, service stations, dry cleaning establishments, oil refineries, and many other industries. In general, aliphatic hydrocarbons are not considered to be hazardous if the concentration is less than 20 percent of the lower inflammable limit, although such a high concentration ($2,000 \times 10^{-6}$) in the case of gasoline may produce unpleasant effects on the human system.

Benzene and other aromatic hydrocarbons are used extensively for solvent extraction purposes. They often occur locally in the air at relatively high concentrations where they can be quite a health hazard. The concentration of aromatic hydrocarbons in city air is probably generally less than 0.1×10^{-6} although some aromatic hydrocarbons are present in automobile exhaust gases.

10.2.2 Secondary pollutants

Secondary pollutants are photochemical oxidants and atmospheric acids formed in the atmosphere due to solar energy-activated reactions of less harmful materials.

1. Photochemical oxidants

Photochemical oxidants are products of secondary atmospheric reactions driven by solar energy. One of the most important of these is ozone (O_3). Ozone is a strong oxidant and can destroy lung tissue and chlorophyll in plants. Other photochemical oxidants include peroxyacetyl nitrate (PAN) and acrolein, both of which are strong oxidants and can damage materials. PAN is also a severe eye irritant.

2. Atmospheric acids

Atmospheric acids occurs when gases such as sulfur acid and nitric acid react in the atmosphere with water, oxygen, and other chemicals to form various acidic compounds. Sunlight increases the rate of most of these reactions. The result is a mild solution of sulfuric acid and nitric acid. Atmospheric acids can occur naturally, for example lightning, volcanoes and so on, but most derive from coal burning and the use of the internal combustion engine.

10.3 Effects of Air Pollution on Human Health

In Bhopal, India, in December 1984, a release of methyl isocyanate from a pesticide plant killed about 2,500 people. Similar leakages of hydrogen sulfide from natural gas processing plants have killed hundreds of people. These tragic events attract wide attention. Normally, they are not considered air pollution events, but rather industrial accidents. The damages to human health caused by air pollution are of a very different type. The materials involved are rarely as toxic as methyl isocyanate or hydrogen sulfide. They are generally not released in concentrations nearly as high as those that cause such disasters. Their effects normally do not result from a single exposure (methyl isocyanate and hydrogen sulfide can kill in a minute or two), but from repeated exposure to low concentrations for long periods.

Table 10.1 lists the air pollutants that are regulated in the United States in 1998 because exposure to them is harmful to human health. The majority of the air pollution efforts in the United States (and most of this book) is devoted to the control of the pollutants on this list. Extensive, detailed reviews of the health effects of air pollutants are regularly published. The rest of this section presents some basic ideas about the health effects of these pollutants.

Table 10.1 Air pollutants believed dangerous to human health and currently regulated in the United States

Pollutants regulated by National Ambient Air Quality Standards (NAAQS) as described in 40CFR50 (as of July 1, 1998). These are called criteria pollutants because before the standards were issued, documents called Air Quality Criteria were issued.

Sulfur oxides

Fine particulate matter

Carbon monoxide

Ozone

Nitrogen dioxide

Chapter 10 Air Pollution

续 Table 10.1

Lead

Pollutants regulated by National Emission Standards for Hazardous Air Pollutants (NESHAP) as described in 40CFR61 (as of July 1, 1998). These are called hazardous air pollutants or air taxies.

Asbestos

Benzene

Beryllium

Coke oven emissions

Inorganic arsenic

Mercury

Radionuclides

Vinyl chloride

The Clean Air Amendments of 1990 expanded this list to 189 chemicals. The regulations for those in addition to the above 8 are currently in the regulatory pipeline.

At least since the time of Paracelsus (1493—1541), people have known that it is meaningless to speak of any substance as harmful unless we specify how much of the substance is administered. He said, "There is poison in everything and no thing is without poison. It is the dose that makes it harmful or not." The same is true of air pollution. To make any meaningful statements about air pollution effects on human health, we must consider the dosages people receive, that is

$$\text{Dosage} = \int (\text{concentration in air breathed})\, d(\text{time})$$

Current interest in air pollution and health is mostly directed at long-term, low-concentration exposures (which lead to chronic effects). Short-term, high-concentration exposures (which lead to acute effects) occur only in industrial accidents (such as the Bhopal tragedy) or air pollution emergency episodes; the latter occurred occasionally in the past, but are now very rare in countries with modem pollution control regulations.

To determine what dosage is harmful, we wish to construct a dose-response curve. Such a curve can be plotted only for individual pollutants, not for "air pollution in general." (Synergism, the effect of two pollutants together being greater than the sum of the separate effects of the two, may occur; that is believed to be the case with sulfur oxides and fine particles, and perhaps some other pollutant combinations as well.) Figure 10.1 is a dose-response curve for a hypothetical homogeneous population exposed to a single hypothetical pollutant for a specific time period. We know most about dose-response curves from pharmacology, where experimental subjects are regularly given carefully measured doses of experimental pharmaceuticals and their responses are measured. From theory and experiment, we know that for pharmaceuticals, the most common dose-response curve is the no-threshold curve, which passes through the origin.

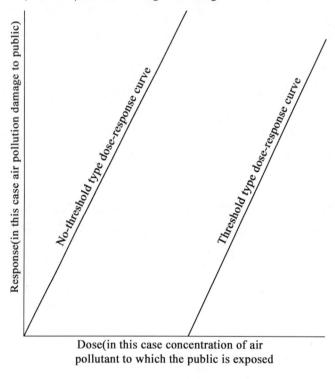

Figure 10.1 Threshold and no-threshold dose-response curves

The straight lines are an admission of ignorance;
we generally do not know the true shapes of these curves

However, in industrial hygiene it has been observed that there is some concentration of pollutants called the threshold value that "represents conditions under which it is believed that nearly all workers may be repeatedly exposed day after day, without adverse effect". These values, called threshold limit values (TLVs), are established by industrial hygiene boards; industrial plants are expected to prevent the exposure of workers to concentrations higher than the TLVs. These TLVs do not represent true no-effect concentrations; rather, they represent concentrations at

Chapter 10 Air Pollution

which the health effects (if they exist) are less than the variation in health of the general populace; hence the "signal" (health effect) is lost in the "noise" of the general health variation of the population. This idea is sketched in Figure 10.2. If the idea of threshold values were literally true, then the true dose-response curves would be like the threshold curve in Figure 10.1. Ghering et al. have presented theoretical grounds for believing that such true thresholds exist. Their theory is illustrated by hydraulic analogy in Figure 10.3. If a first elimination mechanism can handle the entire pollutant input into our bodies, then the second elimination mechanism will not come into play. However, if the first mechanism is saturated, then the second will come into play. If the first mechanism is harmless but the second mechanism creates harmful degradation products within the body or harms some bodily organ, there will be no damage to our bodies as long as the first elimination mechanism can handle the entire input, but harm will result if the input exceeds the capacity of the first elimination mechanism. Under this theory, we would have to

Harmful dosage = $\int [$ (intake rate due to breathing) - (removal rate by first mechanism)$] \, d($time$)$

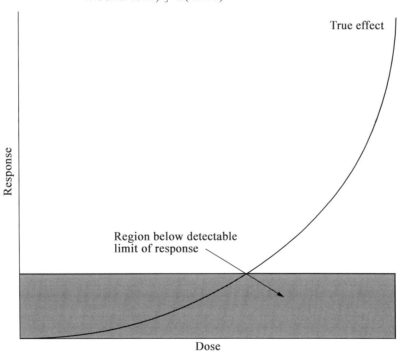

Figure 10.2 The true dose-response situation may be that at low doses the effect is not truly zero but instead is too small for us to detect

(a)　　　　　　　(b)　　　　　　　(c)　　　　　　　(d)

Figure 10.3　A fluid-mechanical analog of the biological mechanism that could result in a true threshold value for a toxic substance

For flow rates less than (b), no flow exits by the higher opening. If the degradation products by the lower route are harmless, and those by the higher are harmful, then the true threshold would correspond to an intake rate equal to that shown in (b)

There are known thresholds for some substances in our diet, such as selenium. Selenium is an essential nutrient; a zero-selenium diet is fatal. Large doses, however, are poisonous; a high-selenium diet is also fatal. Therefore, there must be two thresholds, a lower and a higher one, between which there is a selenium dietary intake level that is harmless (or at least not fatal). Fortunately, the range between the two fatal conditions is fairly wide.

There are theoretical (and some experimental) grounds for believing that there are some substances for which there is no threshold; for such substances, any input is harmful. (Such an input need not cause harm to every person exposed. Instead, it may raise the statistical probability of contracting some disease, e. g. cancer.) In terms of the hydraulic analogy, there is no harmless elimination mechanism (or its effects are so small as to escape experimental detection). Most of the substances believed to have no thresholds are either carcinogens or emitters of ionizing radiation. Establishing the existence or nonexistence of such thresholds experimentally is difficult.

If we wish to establish the dose-response curve for a pollutant, we have three possible approaches: animal experiments, laboratory experiments with humans, and epidemiological studies of human populations.

10.3.1　Animal experiments

A good example of an animal experiment is given in. Two groups of mice (the ozone group and the control group) were simultaneously exposed to an aerosol containing Streptococcus C bacteria, which killed up to 80 percent of the mice. The ozone group had previously been exposed for three hours to various concentrations of ozone; the control group had not been exposed to ozone. The observed mortality values for the ozone and control groups are presented in Table 10.2, and the difference in mortality is plotted against the ozone concentration in Figure 10.4.

From this experiment we observe the following:

(1) It is hard to perform any experiment with living beings and get as good reproducibility as one can with inanimate objects. The control groups in all 10 trials were exposed to what was intended to be the same concentration of bacteria each time. The observed mortality varied from 0 to 15 percent. The data on differences in mortality have significant scatter as well. The negative mortality difference is almost certainly the result of scatter in the experimental data. It is hard to imagine a mechanism by which exposure to 0.07×10^{-6} of ozone would protect mice from subsequent bacterial infection.

Table 10.2 Experimental results from exposure of mice to ozone and then *Streptococcus* C bacteria

Ozone concentration, $\times 10^{-6}$	Percent mortality		
	Control group	Ozone group	Difference
0.52	13	80	67
0.35	0	60	60
0.30	3	40	37
0.20	8	50	42
0.18	0	63	63
0.17	8	45	37
0.10	8	35	37
0.08	15	38	23
0.07	15	35	20
0.07	8	5	-3

(2) Ozone exposure produces a significant effect on mortality at concentrations above about 0.10×10^{-6}, and the effect increases with increasing ozone concentration.

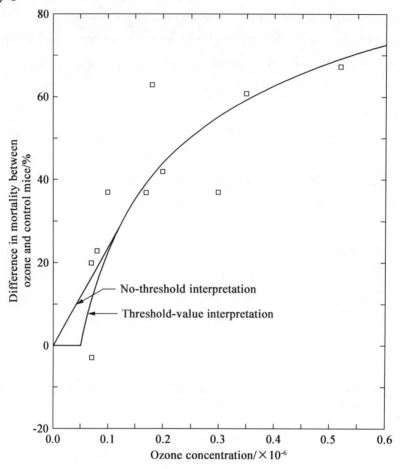

Figure 10.4 Experimental data from Table 10.2 on the difference in mortality between mice exposed to ozone and an unexposed control group, both subsequently exposed to *Streptococcus* bacteria, with two possible interpretations

(3) Here, the air pollution effect was indirect. No mice died as a result of ozone exposure alone. Rather, the ozone, which is a respiratory irritant, presumably irritated the lungs of the exposed mice, making it easier for lethal numbers of bacteria to enter the bloodstream. The authors of the study concluded that the ozone damaged some of the white cells that defend the body against bacterial invasion. If we didn't know the history of the test, we could conclude that exposure to high concentrations of ozone led to increased mortality, but we would probably not know the mechanism of that mortality. This uncertainty about mechanism is common in the epidemiological air pollution studies described in Section 10.3.3. Conversely, if we merely looked at autopsy reports, we would have no way to know which mice

had been exposed to ozone and which not, or that ozone exposure had played any role in their deaths. The autopsy reports would simply say, "Died of bacterial infection."

(4) Although the data scatter is annoying, it is not nearly as great as it would have been if we had used human subjects. The mice in this kind of study are highly inbred so that the genetic variation among them is thousands or millions of times less than that in human populations. Their environment from birth is controlled to make them as similar as possible; the same is not true for humans. Even so, their response shows considerable variation.

(5) From this kind of test, we can estimate the effects on humans of similar exposures. For new drugs not yet in public use, animal experiments are the only way we have of making such estimates. However, what is harmful to one animal may not be harmful to another. For example, before thalidomide (a sedative) was approved for human use, it was extensively tested on mice (including pregnant mice), and showed no harmful effects. In humans, it produced very severe birth defects. Thus, animal tests only suggest what the human health effects of such exposures will be.

(6) These tests measured only acute effects, those seen in a few hours. They give us some guidance about human short-term exposures. Because we are the longest-lived of all mammals, we are concerned with lifetime exposures. Most laboratory animals do not live very long, so it is hard to expose a laboratory animal to some pollutant for more than a year or two. Such short-term tests tell us little about lifetime exposures of humans to the same concentrations of the same pollutants.

(7) This experiment was quick, simple, and cheap. Only small numbers of mice were involved, and the effect considered, death, is easy to detect. To do a similar test for carcinogenicity, one would have to expose mice for much longer and then do an autopsy on each mouse. If one did not know which organ was likely to develop the cancer, one would have to examine every organ of every mouse.

(8) Two interpretations of the data appear in Figure 10.4: a threshold-value interpretation and a no-threshold interpretation. Based on these data alone, one cannot say which of these interpretations (if either) is correct. This flaw is typical of all such animal tests; at high concentrations, the results are rather clear, but at low concentrations the uncertainty and scatter introduced by the variability of even highly inbred mice make it impossible to determine the true shape of the curve. It is

estimated that if one wished to settle completely the threshold or no-threshold question for one substance suspected of being a carcinogen using mice as the experimental animal (which does not necessarily settle the questions for humans), then an experimental program involving at least a million mice would be needed (the "megamouse experiment").

(9) The concentration at which significant effects are seen is near the currently permitted value (NAAQS) of 0.08×10^{-6} in the United States. However, the pathogen exposure that followed the ozone exposure was much more severe than humans normally encounter. It quickly killed up to 15 percent of the control mice.

10.3.2 Short-term exposure of human volunteers

Ample published data show that short-term laboratory exposures of healthy young adults to air pollutant concentrations much higher than those ever measured in the ambient air produce no measurable, irreversible short-term or long-term effects. (Such tests show reversible changes in lung function and other physiological parameters; these changes disappear a few hours after the tests.) However, because we are interested in the effects of long-term exposure, and because we are interested in the health effects not only on healthy young adults but also on the most sensitive members of our society (young children, asthmatics, and the very old), it seems clear that short-term laboratory tests on healthy young adults will not provide the data we need. Such tests are useful for looking for the detailed physiological mechanisms of air pollution damage, but the only way we can ultimately settle health-effect questions is through sophisticated epidemiology.

10.3.3 Epidemiology

Several attempts have been made to do the required epidemiological studies. Perhaps the most interesting is the Community Health and Environmental Surveillance System (CHESS) study. It has received vigorous technical criticism and has been vigorously defended. However, in spite of its technical shortcomings, the general approach of this study is ultimately the one most likely to allow us to construct accurate dose-response curves for air pollutants. In one part of the CHESS study, four cities were selected at various distances from a large copper smelter in the Salt Lake Valley. The cities had a demonstrable gradient of sulfur dioxide concentration because of the prevailing wind patterns, and their different distances from the smelter. The study team attempted to select neighborhoods in each of these cities in which they could match sociological characteristics. For each neighborhood, the study team attempted to measure the health of the populace, with specific emphasis on health problems believed to be influenced by sulfur dioxide (asthma, chronic bronchitis, and lower respiratory disease in children). They then sought a relationship between SO_2 exposure and such diseases. They claim to have demonstrated such a relationship, a conclusion their critics have vigorously denied.

If we assume, for the sake of argument, that their data are valid, we can examine those data to see if they lead to an unambiguous definition of the dose-response relationship for exposure to one specific air pollutant. Figure 10.5 is a plot of the incidence of lower respiratory disease among children as a function of annual average concentration of SO_2 in the four cities. It reveals the following:

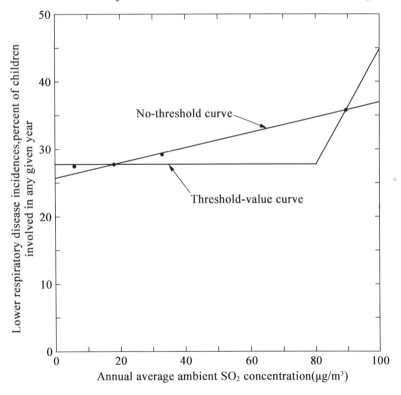

Figure 10.5 Some data from the CHESS study

The points represent study areas in (left to right) Ogden, Salt Lake City, Kearns, and Magna. The SO_2 concentrations are influenced by the distances from a large copper smelter, and by prevailing wind patterns

(1) The health effect considered is not zero for zero pollutant exposure; even in the cleanest environment, a significant fraction of children will have lower respiratory disease in any year. If the curve is of the threshold-value type, then it must proceed horizontally from the zero-exposure value, as shown, until the threshold value is reached, where it will turn upward. The threshold-value curve shown in Figure 10.5 turns upward at 80 $\mu g/m^3$, which is the annual average SO_2 NAAQS in the United States.

(2) The data do not unambiguously support either the threshold-value or the no-threshold interpretation. Given this data set alone, one would be hard pressed to select the better interpretation.

(3) The health effects are plotted versus concentration of SO_2, the most easily measured sulfur oxide. It is far from clear that this is the biologically active agent; it may be serving as a proxy for all sulfur oxides. There is evidence suggesting that the biologically active agent is acid aerosol, created by the deposition of sulfuric acid on fine particles. The CHESS study contains many more data than are shown in Figure 10.5. This particular data set was chosen because it is not complicated by the effect of smoking, which severely complicates all of the adult data.

(4) This location was chosen for study because a 1960s copper smelter emitted large amounts of SO_2 but only small amounts of particulates, producing a sharp gradient in SO_2 concentration without a corresponding gradient in particulate concentration. In most industrial areas SO_2 and particulate concentrations are more or less proportional, so that it is hard to study the effect of one without the other. Since the date of this study, the smelter has reduced its emissions enough that in 1996 the highest annual average ambient SO_2 concentration at any of the four cities shown in Figure 10.5 was about one-tenth of the highest value shown in Figure 10.5. Since 1970 air pollutant emissions from major sources in industrial countries have been reduced enough that the measurements shown in Figure 10.5 are unlikely to be repeated in the United States or other industrial countries.

An alternative epidemiological approach has been to correlate deaths or hospital admissions with measured air pollution concentrations. These can be carried out by looking at historical records (a retrospective study) or by choosing one or more suitable populations and following their health or longevity over time, together with the air pollutant concentrations to which they are exposed (a prospective study). Figure 10.6 shows the results of a retrospective study of the December 1952 London pollution episode. An unusual meteorological situation caused five consecutive days of very low wind speeds over London, England. The concentration of pollutants, mostly derived from coal combustion, increased to values rarely encountered in large cities. Schwartz reported, There was a 2.6-fold increase in deaths in the second week (of December). Increases were seen in all age groups, but the largest relative increases were in ages 65 – 74 (2.8-fold) and ages 75 and over (2.7-fold)... The largest relative increases were seen for bronchitis and emphysema (9.5-fold), tuberculosis (5.5-fold), pneumonia and influenza (4.1-fold), and myocardial degeneration (2.8-fold).

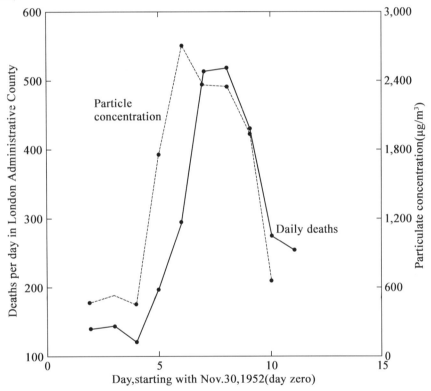

Figure 10.6   Daily death rates and particle concentrations for the December 1952 London pollution episode, after Schwartz

From this report we see:

(1) The observed particle concentrations are very high. Such concentrations have rarely if ever been observed since 1952 in technologically advanced countries.

(2) The increase in deaths followed the increase in particle concentration by a day. It is commonly found in such studies that the concentration the previous day or the average over the previous several days is the best predictor of the daily death

rate.

(3) Other pollutants were present, but statistical analysis of the data shows a better correlation with particulate concentrations than with other pollutant concentrations or combinations of concentrations.

(4) Most of the deaths were not of healthy young persons. Rather they were of susceptible persons, mostly older persons with pre-existing respiratory or circulatory problems. The air pollution episode did not kill them, but rather hastened their deaths or shortened their lives.

Figure 10.7 shows the results of a prospective study of mortality. Large groups (1,200 to 1,600) or participants were selected in six cities. For 14 to 16 years their health and survival were measured, along with concentrations of pollutants in the six cities. The survival rate (fraction of the original study population still living) was highest in the least polluted cities. Figure 10.7 plots the ratio of the annual death rate in each of the cities to that in the cleanest city (Portage, WI). This ratio is obviously 1.00 for Portage, increasing to 1.26 for Steubenville. This study, by the highly respected air pollution group at the Harvard School of Public Health, was one of the major bases for the change in U.S. particulate standards in 1997. From the study we see:

(1) The death rate, adjusted for smoking and some other factors, seems to be linearly proportional to the fine particle concentration (particles with diameters < 2.5 μ). Other air pollutant concentrations or combinations of them did not correlate the mortality data as well.

(2) There does not appear to be any threshold.

(3) The concentrations are quite low. The values are not directly comparable to those in Figure 10.6 because of different measuring methods, but using the best estimates of the correspondence of those methods, one concludes the peak value of $\approx 2,500$ $\mu g/m^3$ on Figure 10.6 would correspond to about 1,500 $\mu g/m^3$ on Figure 10.7. However, the value on Figure 10.7 is an annual average, and those are typically about one-third of the highest-day value, so the proper ratio between the highest values on the two figures is roughly $[1500/(30 \times 3)] \approx 17$.

(4) Figure 10.7 is a comparison of annual death rates as a function of particle concentration whereas Figure 10.6 is of daily death rates. Various statistical studies have shown that the effect is similar over most studies, both prospective and retrospective. The finding is that an increase in particle concentration of 100 $\mu g/m^3$

causes an increase of about 6% in both the annual and the daily death rates.

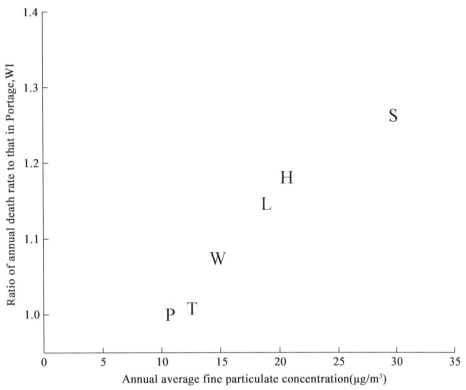

**Figure 10.7 Ratio of death rates to that in Portage, WI,
as a function of fine particle concentration**

P = Portage, WI; T = Topeka, KA; W = Watertown, MA;
L = St. Louis, MO; H = Harriman, TN; S = Steubenville, OH

The two previously reported studies were of death rates (mortality). Other studies concern sicknesses (morbidity). The results are similar; for example, Schwartz reports the results of a... fortuitous natural experiment. Pope... examined hospitalization for respiratory illnesses in children in three adjoining counties in Utah-Utah County, Cache County and Salt Lake County. All had similar housing and demographic patterns. However, in the mid 1980s, the rate of hospitalization for respiratory illness in children in Utah County was approximately twice as great as that in the two adjoining counties. Utah County had an integrated steel mill in a valley subject to temperature inversions. In August 1986, the steel mill shut down due to a strike. It remained closed for 13 months. In that period the rate of hospitalization of children for respiratory conditions in Utah County fell dramatically and was indistinguishable from the rate in the neighboring counties. When the steel mill reopened, the rate of childhood hospitalization for respiratory conditions grew in Utah

County and reached a level about twice as high as that in the adjoining counties once more.

(The steel mill changed owners and has significantly reduced its emissions since 1986—1987. The annual average inhalable particle concentration in Utah County in 1995—1996 was 64 penent of the concentration in 1988—1989.)

These epidemiological studies are all difficult, and their results are subject to challenge. Most require analyzing the data statistically and adjusting the data to account for extraneous variables like smoking, accidental deaths, epidemics, and the like. Often the results are plausible, but of only modest statistical significance. They almost never lead to results as unambiguous as those in Figure 10.4 and 10.6. Nonetheless, they appear to be the best measures we have of the effects of air pollutants on human health, at concentrations to which human populations are regularly exposed.

New Words

barbeque	n. 可携带的烧烤架　vt. 烧烤
charcoal	n. 木炭,炭
Chlorofluorocarbon（CFC）	n. 氟氯烃化合物
depletion	n. 弄空,耗尽,竭尽,[医]衰竭
exhaust	n. 排气管
inert	adj. [化学]惰性的
inversion	n. [气]逆温
noxious	adj. 有害的,有毒的
pose	vt. 使摆姿势,提出,造成
radon	n. [化]氡
stagnation	n. 停滞,沉滞,不流动
stratosphere	n. 等温层,平流层
soot	n. 煤烟,油烟
aerolein	n. [化学]丙烯醛
aliphatic	adj. [化学]脂肪族的
asphyxiation	n. 窒息
carcinogenicity	n. 致癌性,致癌作用
chlorophyll	n. [植物]叶绿素
designation	n. 指明,选派,任命,指示

drowsiness	*n.* 睡意,假寐,困倦
hemogolobin	*n.* 红血球素,血红素
hydrocarbon	*n.* 碳氢化合物
inflammable	*adj.* 易燃的,易怒的,性情暴躁的
irritant	*adj.* 刺激的,有刺激性的
peroxyacetyl nitrate (PAN)	*n.* [化学] 硝酸过氧化乙酰
refinery	*n.* 提炼厂,精炼厂
remnant	*n.* 残余,剩余物,残留

Chapter 11　Solid Waste

11.1　Solid Waste Problems

Since the beginning, humankind has been generating waste, be it the bones and other parts of animals they slaughter for their food or the wood they cut to make their carts. With the progress of civilization, the waste generated became of a more complex nature. At the end of the 19th century the industrial revolution saw the rise of the world of consumers. Not only did the air get more and more polluted but the earth itself became more polluted with the generation of nonbiodegradable solid waste. The increase in population and urbanization was also largely responsible for the increase in solid waste.

Each household generates garbage or waste day in and day out. It seems that we no longer need or do not have any further use for fall in the category of waste, and we tend to throw them away. There are different types of solid waste depending on their source. Solid waste can be classified into three types depending on their source: ① Household waste is generally classified as municipal waste; ② Industrial waste as hazardous waste; ③ Biomedical waste or hospital waste as infectious waste.

11.1.1　Municipal solid waste

Municipal solid waste consists of household waste, construction and demolition debris, sanitation residue, and waste from streets. This garbage is generated mainly from residential and commercial complexes. With rising urbanization and change in lifestyle and food habits, the amount of municipal solid waste has been increasing rapidly and its composition changing. In 1947 cities and towns in India generated an estimated 6 million tones of solid waste; in 1997 it was about 48 million tones. More than 25% of the municipal solid waste is not collected at all; 70% of the Indian cities

Chapter 11 Solid Waste

lack adequate capacity to transport it and there are no sanitary landfills to dispose of the waste. The existing landfills are neither well equipped nor well managed and are not lined properly to protect against contamination of soil and groundwater.

Over the last few years, the consumer market has grown rapidly leading to products being packed in cans, aluminum foils, plastics, and other such nonbiodegradable items that cause incalculable harm to the environment. In India, some municipal areas have banned the use of plastics and they seem to have achieved success. For example, today one will not see a single piece of plastic in the entire district of Ladakh where the local authorities imposed a ban on plastics in 1998. Other states should follow the example of this region and ban the use of items that cause harm to the environment. One positive note is that in many large cities, shops have begun packing items in reusable or biodegradable bags. Certain biodegradable items can also be composted and reused. In fact proper handling of the biodegradable waste will considerably lessen the burden of solid waste that each city has to tackle.

There are different categories of waste generated, each take their own time to degenerate (as illustrated in the table below).

Table 11.1 the type of litter and the approximate time of its degeneration

Num	Type of litter	Approximate time it takes to degenerate
1	Organic waste(vegetable, fruit peels, leftover foodstuff, ect.)	A week or two
2	Paper	10 ~ 30 days
3	Cotton cloth	2 ~ 5 months
4	Wood	10 ~ 15 years
5	Woolen items	1 years
6	Matels	100 ~ 500 years
7	Plastics	Undetermined
8	Glass	Undetermined

11.1.2 Hazardous waste

Industrial and hospital waste is considered hazardous as they may contain toxic substances. Certain types of household waste are also hazardous. Hazardous wastes could be highly toxic to humans, animals, and plants; are corrosive, highly inflammable, or explosive; and react when exposed to certain things e. g. gases. India generates around 7 million tones of hazardous wastes every year, most of which is concentrated in four states: Andhra Pradesh, Bihar, Uttar Pradesh, and Tamil Nadu. Household wastes that can be categorized as hazardous waste include old batteries, shoe polish, paint tins, old medicines, and medicine bottles.

Hospital waste contaminated by chemicals used in hospitals is considered hazardous. These chemicals include formaldehyde and phenols, which are used as disinfectants, and mercury, which is used in thermometers or equipment that measure blood pressure. Most hospitals in India do not have proper disposal facilities for these hazardous wastes.

In the industrial sector, the major generators of hazardous waste are the metal, chemical, paper, pesticide, dye, refining, and rubber goods industries. Direct exposure to chemicals in hazardous waste such as mercury and cyanide can be fatal.

11.1.3　Hospital waste

Hospital waste is generated during the diagnosis, treatment, or immunization of human beings or animals or in research activities in these fields or in the production or testing of biological. It may include wastes like sharps, soiled waste, disposables, anatomical waste, cultures, discarded medicines, chemical wastes, etc.. These are in the form of disposable syringes, swabs, bandages, body fluids, human excreta, etc.. This waste is highly infectious and can be a serious threat to human health if not managed in a scientific and discriminate manner. It has been roughly estimated that of the 4 kg of waste generated in a hospital at least 1 kg would be infected.

Surveys carried out by various agencies show that the health care establishments in India are not giving due attention to their waste management. After the notification of the Bio-medical Waste (Handling and Management) Rules, 1998, these establishments are slowly streamlining the process of waste segregation, collection, treatment, and disposal. Many of the larger hospitals have either installed the treatment facilities or are in the process of doing so.

11.2　Treatment and Disposal of Municipal Waste

As cities are growing in size with a rise in the population, the amount of waste generated is increasing becoming unmanageable. The local corporations have adapted different methods for the disposal of waste—open dumps, landfills, sanitary landfills, and incineration plants. One of the important methods of waste treatment is composting.

11.2.1　Open dumps

Open dumps refer to uncovered areas that are used to dump solid waste of all kinds. The waste is untreated, uncovered, and not segregated. It is the breeding ground for flies, rats, and other insects that spread disease. The rainwater run-off from these dumps contaminates nearby land and water thereby spreading disease. In some countries, open dumps are being phased out.

11.2.2　Landfills

Landfills are generally located in urban areas where a large amount of waste is generated and has to be dumped in a common place. Unlike an open dump, it is a pit that is dug in the ground. The garbage is dumped and the pit is covered thus preventing the breeding of flies and rats. At the end of each day, a layer of soil is scattered on top of it and some mechanism, usually on earth-moving equipment is used to compress the garbage, which now forms a cell. Thus, every day, garbage is dumped and becomes a cell. After the landfill is full, the area is covered with a thick layer of mud and the site can thereafter be developed as a parking lot or a park.

Landfills have many problems. All types of waste is dumped in landfills and when water seeps through them it gets contaminated and in turn pollutes the surrounding area. This contamination of groundwater and soil through landfills is known as leaching.

11.2.3　Sanitary landfills

An alternative to landfills which will solve the problem of leaching to some extent is a sanitary landfill which is more hygienic and built in a methodical manner. These are lined with materials that are impermeable such as plastics and clay, and are also built over impermeable soil. Constructing sanitary landfills is very costly and they are having their own problems. Some authorities claim that often the plastic liner develops cracks as it reacts with various chemical solvents present in the waste.

The rate of decomposition in sanitary landfills is also extremely variable. This can be due to the fact that less oxygen is available as the garbage is compressed very tightly. It has also been observed that some biodegradable materials do not decompose in a landfill. Another major problem is the development of methane gas, which occurs when little oxygen is present, i.e. during anaerobic decomposition. In some countries, the methane being produced from sanitary landfills is tapped and sold as fuel.

11.2.4 Incineration plants

This process of burning waste in large furnaces is known as incineration. In these plants the recyclable material is segregated and the rest of the material is burnt. At the end of the process all that is left behind is ash. During the process some of the ash floats out with the hot air. This is called fly ash. Both the fly ash and the ash that is left in the furnace after burning have high concentrations of dangerous toxins such as dioxins and heavy metals. Disposing of this ash is a problem. The ash that is buried at the landfills leaches the area and cause severe contamination.

Burning garbage is not a clean process as it produces tonnes of toxic ash and pollutes the air and water. A large amount of the waste that is burnt here can be recovered and recycled. In fact, at present, incineration is kept as the last resort and is used mainly for treating the infectious waste.

11.2.5 Composting

Organic matter can be recycled by the method of composting, one of the oldest forms of disposal. It is the natural process of decomposition of organic waste that yields manure or compost, which is very rich in nutrients. Composting is a biological process in which micro-organisms, mainly fungi and bacteria, convert degradable organic waste into humus like substance. This finished product, which looks like soil, is high in carbon and nitrogen and is an excellent medium for growing plants. The process of composting ensures the waste that is produced in the kitchens is not carelessly thrown and left to rot. It recycles the nutrients and returns them to the soil as nutrients. Apart from being clean, cheap, and safe, composting can significantly reduce the amount of disposable garbage. The organic fertilizer can be used instead of chemical fertilizers and is better specially when used for vegetables. It increases the soil's ability to hold water and makes the soil easier to cultivate. It helped the soil retain more of the plant nutrients.

Vermi-composting has become very popular in the last few years. In this method, worms are added to the compost. These help to break the waste and the added excreta of the worms makes the compost very rich in nutrients. To make a compost pit, you have to select a cool, shaded corner of the garden or the school compound and dig a pit, which ideally should be 3 feet deep. This depth is convenient for aerobic composting as the compost has to be turned at regular intervals in this process. Preferably the pit should be lined with granite or brick to prevent nitrite pollution of the subsoil water, which is known to be highly toxic. Each time organic matter is added to the pit it should be covered with a layer of dried leaves or a thin layer of soil which allows air to enter the pit thereby preventing bad odour. At the end of 45 days, the rich pure organic matter is ready to be used.

New Words

anatomical	*adj.* 解剖的,解剖学的
nonbiodegradable	*adj.* 不可生物降解的
cyanide	*n.* [化学] 氰化物
phenol	*n.* [化学] 苯酚
demolition	*n.* 破坏 *pl.* 废墟
sanitation	*n.* 卫生,卫生设施
lessen	*vt.* 减轻,减少
slaughter	*n.* 屠宰
immunization	*n.* 免疫作用,有免疫力
landfill	*n.* 垃圾填埋场
formaldehyde	*n.* [化学] 甲醛
compost	*n.* 混合肥料,混合物
phase	*n.* 阶段,局面,[物] 相位

pit	n. 坑,壕沟,地洞
disposal	n. 处理　vt. 使凹陷,储存于坑内
dump	n. 垃圾堆
sanitary	adj. 卫生的,环境卫生的
hygienic	n. 卫生学
subsoil	n. 下层土,底土
incineration	n. 焚烧,焚化,煅烧
leaching	n. 滤出,渗滤,流失
manure	n. 肥料,粪　vt. 施肥于

Part 3　Writing

Chapter 12　The Abstract

12.1　The Abstract and Its Function

近年来,英文已成为各国间进行科技交流的主要工具。为了便于交流,许多以中文发表的科技论文、研究生学位论文、本科生论文都要求有长短不同的英文摘要。那么,什么是摘要,如何才能写好摘要呢?

摘要是以提供论文内容梗概为目的,不加评论和补充解释,简明确切地记述论文重要内容的短文。科技论文摘要是论文的缩影,其作用是简明扼要地介绍论文的内容,展示论文内容足够的信息,体现论文的创新性,说明研究的目的、方法、研究成果和最终结论,应放在论文正文之前。摘要是读者是否继续阅读全文的重要依据,读者阅读正文前一般先读摘要,如果摘要不能引起读者的兴趣,读者就不会再读正文。

一篇好的英文摘要应满足如下几点要求:

(1)摘要要具有独立性、完整性,要使读者未读论文全文前能获得必要的信息。它是可以独立使用的一篇短文,因此要忠实于正文,不能包含正文中没有的信息。

(2)摘要应精练,只陈述所得的结果,不宜列举例证,无需引用参考文献,不包含讨论和推理。

(3)除极特殊情况外,摘要中一般不用图、表、化学结构式、非公知公用的符号和术语。

(4)宜以第三人称书写,避免使用第一人称做主语。

(5)应与中文摘要内容一致,译文确切,无语法错误。

(6)应注意包含3~5个关键词(Keywords)。

(7)要正确使用动词时态,英文摘要中最常用的时态是一般现在时、一般过去时和现在完成时。一般用过去时态叙述作者所做的工作,用现在时态叙述作者得出的结果、结论。

(8)对那些已经为大众所熟悉的缩写词,可以直接使用,对于那些仅为同行所熟悉的缩略语,应在题目、文摘或关键词中至少出现一次全称。

(9)英文摘要的长度一般为100~300词,不同的学术期刊对论文摘要的长度一般有严格要求。

12.2 The Classification of Abstract

摘要可分为描述性摘要、信息性摘要和综合性摘要三大类。

12.2.1 Indicative abstract

描述性摘要(亦称指示性摘要)简要概述论文的内容,由于只是对论文的主要观点、涉及范围以及结论做概述,不包含具体的数据和结果,不涉及实质问题,因此,它很难代替论文全文。研究性论文一般不采用这类摘要,而评论性文章、综述性论文、数学计算和理论推导等一般采用这类摘要。这类摘要在时态上多采用一般现在时或一般过去时被动语态,简明扼要。

E. g. 1: Several issues faced in the process of bioremediation were discussed in this paper, which are included as below: the principal and condition for the introducing of foreigner microbial; mechanisms of suitability for microorganisms in the bioremediation process and the factors that influenced the degradation of pollutants; the correlations between the concentration of pollutants and their bioremediation; the secondary pollutants in the process of degradation of organic chemicals; the technology amplification of bioremediation technique situ or/and in situ; the leaching process of contaminants; the eco-toxicological diagnosis and evaluation for bioremediation technology and so on in order to enhance the realization for problems existed in the process of bioremediation and make it possible for more effective application of the bioremediation technology.

E. g. 2: The Construction of water environmental management system is a complicated systemic engineering. Even if in the developed country, the model of water environmental management was changed continuously and perfected gradually along with the developing of knowledge level. In this paper, the information on water environmental management of international representational countries was collected, for example America, English, France, Holland, Canada, Australia, Russia, Japan, Korea, Israel and India , and analyzed the system and model which adopted by these country in degree of nation, river basin and region. At the same time, the indigestion of the water management system of our country was analyzed too, therefore, the basic principles which the reformation of water environmental management of our country were proposed at the end.

E. g. 3: Agroecosystem functional assessment indicators provide a necessary bridge between decision-makers and scientists. The development of acceptable indicators, however, remains a difficult task because the current knowledge and understanding of ecosystems is not sufficient to allow an objective assessment of all ecosystem functions. These difficulties were summarized from three perspectives. First, there are difficulties in individual function assessment. Of the four functions associated with agroecosystems—energy flow, materials cycling, information flow and value flow-data on material cycling remain difficult to obtain and the indicators relatively immature. Secondly, there are difficulties of integration. During the assessment process, the integration of the agroecosystem functions remains the biggest obstacle. Until now, there has been no practical or effective methodology established to resolve the problem. At present, the makeshift approach has been to weight the various indicators and then add them together. Thirdly, there is the problem of obscure concepts and concept confusion. When assessments of agroecosystems are conducted, concepts such as structure, function, benefit, and resource utilization are used extensively. To date, no logical relationship either real or implied has been developed between any of these concepts. Are they causes and results such that the relationship between them is linear, or are they independent from one another such that the relationship is parallel? Thus far, the essence of this question is yet to be explored.

E. g. 4: Ecological construction and restoration for sustainable development are now a driving paradigm. It is increasingly recognized that ecological principles, especially landscape ecology theory, are not only necessary but also essential to maintain the long-term sustainability worldwide. Key landscape ecology principles and element, structure and process, dynamics, heterogeneity, hierarchies, connectivity, place and time were reviewed, and use Beijing area as a case study to illustrate how these principles might be applied to ecological construction and restoration, to eventually achieve sustainability. An example to more effectively incorporate the ecological principles in sustainable planning in China was presented.

E. g. 5: Magnetotactic bacteria can orient and migrate along geomagnetic field lines because of their intracellular single-domain magnetic nano-crystal particles with biomembrane bounded, which are referred as magnetosomes. Magnetite Fe_3O_4 is the main chemical component of magnetosomes characterized by the high chemical purity, fine grain size uniformity, and good biocompatibility, which can be used as a new kind of nano-magnetic materials applied in many fields of biochemistry, magnetic materials, clinical medicine and wastewater treatment and so on. Magnetosome formation is the mineralization process under strict biochemical mechanisms control, including four steps: iron accumulation, membrane formation, transportation and controlled biomineralization of Fe_3O_4. In this paper, the characteristics of magnetotactic bacteria, chemical composition, structure, synthesis conditions and mechanisms, magnetism, separation and purification, the applications of the nano-magnetic particles are summarized and reviewed. The main problems to be resolved and the prospects of magnetosomes are also presented.

E.g.6: Over the past few decades, researchers have established artificial enzymes as highly stable and low-cost alternatives to natural enzymes in a wide range of applications. A variety of materials including cyclodextrins, metal complexes, porphyrins, polymers, dendrimers and biomolecules have been extensively explored to mimic the structures and functions of naturally occurring enzymes. Recently, some nanomaterials have been found to exhibit unexpected enzyme-like activities, and great advances have been made in this area due to the tremendous progress in nano-research and the unique characteristics of nanomaterials. To highlight the progress in the field of nanomaterial-based artificial enzymes (nanozymes), this review discusses various nanomaterials that have been explored to mimic different kinds of enzymes. We cover their kinetics, mechanisms and applications in numerous fields, from biosensing and immunoassays, to stem cell growth and pollutant removal. We also summarize several approaches to tune the activities of nanozymes. Finally, we make comparisons between nanozymes and other catalytic materials (other artificial enzymes, natural enzymes, organic catalysts and nanomaterial-based catalysts) and address the current challenges and future directions.

12.2.2　Informative abstract

信息性摘要概括论文的目的、研究所采用的方法、主要研究结果和结论等,对于最佳条件、成功的数据及误差范围、结论及适用范围均如实给出。这类摘要的着眼点放在具体的条件和数据上,反映了论文的基本面貌,可以说是科技论文主要内容的缩影,可以被单独引用。在时态上可用一般现在时和一般过去时的被动语态,也可以使用现在完成时的被动语态。句子之间没有必然的联系,一句话说明一件事。国际会议论文和实验性、技术性较强的论文常采用此类摘要。

Chapter 12 The Abstract

E. g. 1: A new method of ultrasonic irritation was applied to decompose sodium dodecyl benzene sulphonate (SDBS) in aqueous solution. Effects of sonication time, ultrasonic frequency, ultrasonic power, ultrasonic intensity, probe diameter, initial pH value and cavitating gas on SDBS degradation efficiency were experimentally studied. The results show that SDBS degradation efficiencies increase linearly with sonication time in the first-order kinetics. Influence of ultrasonic frequency on SDBS degradation in low frequency ranges is insignificant. With increase of ultrasonic power, intensity and probe diameters, SDBS degradation efficiency increases to a maximum value of 42.5%. Effect of initial pH value on SDBS degradation is significant and acidic condition is more favorable for the reaction. The attendance of selected cavitating gases is good for SDBS degradation; their contribution order is $Ar > O_2 > N_2$.

E. g. 2: The photocatalytic degradation of aniline in water was studied in annular photoreactor with UV lamp as light source and titanium dioxide immobilized on porous nickel as catalysts. The results showed that the kinetic of photocatalytic degradation rate of aniline can be described by Langmuir – Hinshelwood equation. The effects of the concentration of aniline, pH, flow rate, concentration of oxygen and external addition of H_2O_2 were also investigated and the results were explained.

E. g. 3: Biofiltration technique for disposing ammonia-contaminated gas streams was investigated. The effects of retention time, gas introducing ways and initial concentration of ammonia on the ammonia removal efficiency were studied. The ammonia removal efficiency was higher than 95% when the inlet ammonia concentration was 15.2, 75.9 or 152.0 $mg(NH_3)/m^3$, and the ammonia elimination rate was 0.020, 0.078 or 0.156 $g/(kg \cdot d)$. The experimental results indicated that the optimum gas introducing way is counter flow and the preferable retention time was 32 s.

E. g. 4: Thirteen pure strains that possessed high methyl red (MR)-decolorizing ability were isolated from dye-contaminated water. Each isolate was identified by 16S rDNA sequencing. The results reveal that all of the isolated strains were facultative anaerobic bacteria. Two novel bacterial consortia (AE and AN), which could decolo-rize MR under aerobic and anaerobic conditions, respectively, were developed. Azo dye decolorization rate was significantly higher with the use of consortia compared to that with the use of individual strains. Both of the consortia can decolo-rize different azo dyes effectively in a short time, and tolerate MR with high concentrations. To provide further insight into the microbial diversity of the bacteria consortia under aerobic and anaerobic conditions, polymerase chain reaction-denaturing gradient gel electrophoresis (PCR-DGGE) analyses were performed. PCR-DGGE profiles revealed that the microbial community had changed significantly with varying initial concentrations of MR. Phylogenetic analysis indicated that microbial populations in the aerobic compartment belong to Klebsiella, Buttiauxella and Bacillus, whereas Klebsiella, Escherichia, Bacillus and Clostridium were present in the anaerobic compartment. Klebsiella, which was the majority genus in both of the consortia, may play an important role in azo dye removal.

E. g. 5: Aerobic granular sludge was cultivated in sequencing batch airlift reactors (SBAR) at 25, 30, and 35 ℃, respectively. The effect of temperature on the granules characteristics was analyzed and the microbial community structures of the granules were probed using scanning electron microscope (SEM) and polymerase chain reaction-denaturing gradient gel electrophoresis (PCR-DGGE). The results showed that 30 ℃ is optimum for matured granule cultivation, where the granules had a more compact structure, better settling ability and higher bioactivity, the oxygen utilization rate (OUR) reached 1.14 mg O_2/(g MLVSS · min) with COD removal rate of 97% and TP removal rate of 75%. The removal efficiency of NH_3-N increased from 68.5% to 87.5% along with the temperature increment from 25 to 35 ℃. The DGGE profiles revealed that the microbial community structure at 25 ℃ showed the least similarity with those at other temperatures. The sequencing results indicated that the majority of dominant microbes belonged to *Actinobacteria* and *Proteobacterium*, *Thermomonas* sp., *Ottowiasp* and *Curtobacterium ammoniigenes* might play important roles at different temperatures, respectively.

E. g. 6: A thermo-alkali-stable laccase gene from Bacillus licheniformis was cloned and expressed in *Pichia pastoris*. The recombinant laccase was secreted into the culture medium with a maximum activity of 227.9 U/L. The purified laccase is a monomeric glycoprotein, and its molecular weight was estimated to be 65 kDa on SDS-PAGE after deglycosylation. Optimal enzyme activity was observed at pH 6.2 and 70 ℃ with syringaldazine as substrate. The recombinant laccase was highly stable in the pH range 7–9 after 10 days at 30 ℃. The enzyme displayed remarkable thermostability at 50–70 ℃, with a half-life of inactivation at 70 ℃ of 6.9 h. It also exhibited high tolerance to NaCl and organic solvents like the native spore laccase. The purified laccase could rapidly decolorize reactive blue 19, reactive black 5 and indigo carmine in the presence of acetosyringone. More than 93% of the tested dyes were decolorized in 4 h at pH 9.0.

E.g.7: Aerobic granular sludge was cultivated by using different kinds of seed sludge in sequencing batch airlift reactor. The influence of seed sludge on physical and chemical properties of granular sludge was studied; the microbial community structure was probed by using scanning electron microscope and polymerase chain reaction-denaturing gradient gel electrophoresis (PCR-DGGE). The results showed that seed sludge played an important role on the formation of aerobic granules. Seed sludge taken from beer wastewater treatment plant (inoculum A) was more suitable for cultivating aerobic granules than that of sludge from municipal wastewater treatment plant (inoculum B). Cultivated with inoculum A, large amount of mature granules formed after 35 days operation, its SVI reached 32.75 mL/g, and SOUR of granular sludge was beyond 1.10 mg/(g·min). By contrast, it needed 56 days obtaining mature granules using inoculum B. DGGE profiles indicated that the dominant microbial species in mature granules were 18 and 11 OTU when inoculum A and B were respectively employed as seed sludge. The sequencing results suggested that dominant species in mature granules cultivated by inoculum A were *Paracoccus* sp., *Devosia hwasunensi*, *Pseudoxanthomonas* sp., while the dominant species were *Lactococcusra ffinolactisand*, *Pseudomonas* sp. in granules developed from inoculum B.

E.g.8: In order to evaluate the influence of microbial community structure of seed sludge on the properties of aerobic nitrifying granules, aerobic nitrifying granules were cultivated with different seed sludge, the variation of microbial community and the dominant bacterial groups that impact nitrogen removal efficiency of the aerobic nitrifying granules were analyzed and identified using 16S rDNA sequence and denaturing gradient gel electrophoresis (DGGE) profiles. The results presented here demonstrated that the influence of community structure of seed sludge on the properties of aerobic nitrifying granules was remarkable, and the aerobic nitrifying granules cultivated by activated sludge from beer wastewater treatment plant possess better performances with stable sludge volume index (SVI) value of 20 mL/g, high extracellular polymeric substance (EPS) content of 183.3 mg/L, high $NH_4^+ - N$ removal rate of 89.42% and abundant microbial population with 10 dominant bacterial groups, indicating that the activated sludge with abundant communities is suitable to be used as seed sludge in culturing aerobic nitrifying granules.

E.g.9: Prussian-blue (PB)-modified Fe_2O_3 magnetic nanoparticles (PBMNPs) were successfully synthesized based on electric interactions between negatively charged $[Fe(CN)_6]^{4-}$ and positively charged Fe_2O_3 nanoparticles. The in situ PB coating was generated by the coordinating reaction between the adsorbed $[Fe(CN)_6]^{4-}$ and the ferric ions on the surface of Fe_2O_3 NPs. The as-prepared PBM-NPs were characterized by FT-IR, XRD, TEM, and used to remove organic pollutants from aqueous solution, namely, using methylene blue (MB) as model compound. The experimental results showed that the target compound could be removed efficiently from solution over a wide pH range from 3 to 10 in the presence of PBM-NPs as peroxidase-like catalyst and H_2O_2 as oxidant. Under optimal conditions, MB could be removed completely after 120 min of reaction at 298 K; the chemical oxygen demand (COD) removal efficiency and the total organic carbon (TOC) abatement efficiency were 53.6% and 35%, respectively. Furthermore, the PBMNPs catalysts showed high magnetization, temperature tolerance, long-term storage and operational stability, and they could be readily separated from solution by applying an external magnetic field. Finally, a possible reaction mechanism for MB degradation was also discussed.

12.2.3　Indicative and informative abstract

综合性摘要既有描述性内容，又有信息性内容，既提供论文的背景和条件，也有研究的方法和分析，还有具体的数据和结论。这类摘要常见于学位论文和专题研究。下面列举的是几篇综合性摘要。

E.g.1: Land degradation is a consequence stemming from both natural processes and social economic activities. On the bases of analyzing general situation of agricultural land degradation in China, the monetary estimating methods such as market value method and shadow engineering method were used to quantitatively assess the economic loss resulting from land deterioration. Results showed that the economic loss in 1999 was 326.81 billion RMB Yuan, which accounted for 4.1% of GDP in the same year of China. If taking five items namely farmland conversion, soil erosion, salination, decline in reservoir functions, and siltation in waterways and, comparing with that in 1992, the percentage of economic loss to GDP has increased by 1.5 in the only 7 years.

E.g.2: Photocatalytic oxidation (PCO) process is an effective way to deal with organic pollutants in wastewater which could be difficult to be degraded by conventional biological treatment methods. Normally the TiO_2 powder in nanometer size range was directly used as photocatalyst for dye degradation in wastewater. However the titanium dioxide powder was arduous to be recovered from the solution after treatment. In this application, a new form of TiO_2 (i. e. pillar pellets ranging from 2.5 to 5.3 mm long and with a diameter of 3.7 mm) was used and investigated for photocatalytic degradation of textile dye effluent. A test system was built with a flat plate reactor (FPR) and UV light source (blacklight and solar simulator as light source respectively) for investigating the effectiveness of the new form of TiO_2. It was found that the photocatalytic process under this configuration could efficiently remove colours from textile dyeing effluent. Comparing with the TiO_2 powder, the pellet was very easy to recover from the treated solution and can be reused in multiple times without the significant change on the photocatalytic property. The results also showed that to achieve the same photocatalytic performance, the FPR area by pellets was about 91 % smaller than required by TiO_2 powder. At least TiO_2 pellet could be used as an alternative form of photocatalyst in applications for textile effluent treatment process, also other wastewater treatment processes.

E. g. 3: In the system of nitric oxide removal from the flue gas by metal chelate adsorption, it is an obstacle that ferrous adsorbents are easily oxidized by oxygen in the flue gas to ferric counterparts, which are not capable of binding NO. By adding iron metal or electrochemical method, $Fe^{III}(EDTA)$ can be reduced to $Fe^{II}(EDTA)$. However, there are various drawbacks associated with these techniques. The dissimilatory reduction of $Fe^{III}(EDTA)$ with microorganisms in the system of nitric oxide removal by metal Fe^{III} chelate adsorption was investigated. Ammonium salt instead of nitrate was used as the nitrogen source, as nitrates inhibited the reduction of Fe^{III} due to the competition between the two electron acceptors. Supplemental glucose and lactate stimulated the formation of Fe^{II} more than ethanol as the carbon sources. The microorganisms cultured at 50 ℃ were not very sensitive to the other experimental temperature, the reduction percentage of Fe^{III} varied little with the temperature range of 30 – 50 ℃. Concentrated Na_2CO_3 solution was added to adjust the solution pH to an optimal pH range of 6 – 7. The overall results revealed that the dissimilatory ferric reducing microorganisms present in the mix-culture are probably neutrophilic, moderately thermophilic Fe^{III} reducers.

E. g. 4: The atmospheric precipitation plays an important role in influencing the river chemistry of the Dongjiang River. The atmospheric contribution to river water is estimated by reference to Cl concentration called Cl_{ref}. The Cl_{ref} of 41.97 μmol/L represents the highest chloride concentration of the rainwater inputs to river water, thus sea salts are responsible for total Cl concentration of the Dongjiang River. According to the principal compositions of precipitation and river water, two approaches-sea salt correction and precipitation correction were proposed in order to correct the contribution proportions of atmospheric precipitation on the solutes and to calculate chemical weathering rate. The results reflected that the atmospheric contribution ratios fluctuate from 5% to 20% of TDS (total dissolved solids) in the Dongjiang River. As compared with the other world watersheds, the lower dissolved ion contents and high runoff may result in the obvious influence of precipitation on river chemistry in the Dongjiang basin. The major elemental chemistry is mainly controlled by silicate weathering, with the anion HCO_3^- and cation Ca^{2+} and Na^+ dominating the major compositions in this basin. The estimated chemical weathering rate of 15.78 – 23.48 $t/(km^2 \cdot a)$ is only 40% – 60% of a global average in the Dongjiang basin. Certainly, the estimated results are still under correction gradually because the effect of human activities on the precipitation chemistry has never been quantified in detail.

E. g. 5: Accidental collapse resulted from unstable factors is an important technological problem to be solved in sanitary landfill. Microbiological degradation of organic maters in landfill solid waste is an important unstable factor. A landfill reactor was thus manufactured and installed to examine quantitative and population dynamics of microorganisms during degradation of landfill solid waste. It was showed that unstable landfill can be reflected and indicated by microbiological features such as rapidly decreased growth amount of microorganisms, no detection of fungi and actinomyces, and changing the dominant population into methanogenic bacteria and acinetobacter.

12.3　The Abstract Writing

摘要是要用较少的文字传达重要的信息,因此第一句话要高度概括文章的目的、性质、方法乃至重要的成果,然后再写所得到的重要数据、结果或结论。摘要中句子之间没有必然的联系,可以相对独立,一句话说明一件事。

12.3.1　Common topic sentences

摘要中的第一句话即主题句常见的句式有:"A new approach is proposed to..."

Chapter 12　The Abstract

"A new method was developed for..." "This paper describes..." "This paper analyses..." "This paper discusses..." "This paper gives a new approach of..." "This paper investigates..." "... was studied" "... was prepared by..." "... was discussed" "... was presented"等。

常见的谓语动词有：report, study, investigate, present, develop, discuss, show, describe, introduce 等。

E. g. 1: The effect of Profenofos on Phaeodactylum tricornutum and Platymonos helgolandica proliferation and its possible mechanism were studied.

研究了丙溴磷对三角褐指藻和青岛大扁藻生长的影响及其可能的机理。

E. g. 2: This paper investigates the effects of different structures of organic compounds on their sonophotocatalytic degradation.

本文探讨了不同有机化合物结构对超声光催化降解的影响.

E. g. 3: A new method of ultrasonic radiation was developed for decompose sodium dodecyl benzene sulphonate (SDBS) in aqueous solution.

本文报道了一种新的超声辐射降解水体中有机污染物十二烷基苯磺酸钠（SDBS）的方法。

E. g. 4: Relationships between the concentration of PAHs, forms of occurrence in air and traffic intensity, wind velocity, temperature and concentrations of NO_x, SO_2, TSP were discussed .

讨论了大气中 PAHs 的浓度、存在形态与车流量、气温、风速、NO_x、SO_2、总悬浮微粒（TSP）浓度之间的关系。

E. g. 5: Under different sintering temperatures (340 ℃, 440 ℃, 540 ℃, 640 ℃), four TiO_2 particles were prepared.

在不同烧结温度（340 ℃, 440 ℃, 540 ℃, 640 ℃）下制备了 4 种 TiO_2 颗粒。

E. g. 6: A series of composite flocculants polyaluminium chloride (PAC) – polydimethyl diallyammonium chloride (PDMDAAC) was prepared by using PAC with different basicity (B) and PDMDAAC as raw materials.

以具有不同碱化度（B）的聚合氯化铝（PAC）和二甲基二烯丙基氯化铵均聚物（PDMDAAC）为原料，制备出了系列 PAC – PDMDAAC。

E. g. 7: Biofiltration technique for treating H_2S-contaminated gas of lower concentration was investigated.

研究了生物滤塔处理含低浓度 H_2S 恶臭气体的技术。

E. g. 8: A dynamic environmental quality assessment method for wetland sediments is proposed in this paper.

本文提出了一种适用于湿地沉积物的动态环境质量评价方法。

E.g.9: The present study deals with the performance evaluation of the UASB reactor for the treatment of paper mill wastewater.

本研究涉及用于造纸厂废水处理的 UASB 反应器的性能的评估。

E.g.10: A silica gel fractionation procedure for environmental sample extracts, which separates chlorinated hydrocarbons and organophosphorus, pyrethroid pesticides into two groups for subsequent instrumental analysis, was developed in this study.

本文提出了用于环境样品萃取物的硅胶分馏程序。这一程序能将氯化烃和有机磷、拟除虫菊酯除草剂分成两组用于连续仪器分析。

12.3.2 Tense

英语论文摘要中的动词时态的使用原则一般为：实验结果、方法描述等都用现在时态表述；一般用过去时叙述作者所做的工作；叙述从某一时间开始，与现在有直接关系并对目前有影响的事情，用现在完成时；叙述今后的研究和打算、预期的结果、倾向等均用一般将来时。

12.3.3 Ending sentenses

在英文摘要的结尾有时写上作者的结论或建议，下面是一些常见的句式：

E.g.1: The author suggests (recommends, concludes) that...

E.g.2: This article shows that...

E.g.3: It is suggested that...

E.g.4: The author's suggestion (or conclusion) is that...

E.g.5: The author finds it necessary to...

Exercise

请将下面两篇文摘翻译成英文：

(1) 以苯胺及其衍生物为研究对象，探讨了不同有机化合物结构对超声光催化降解的影响，进一步开拓了基于超声波与 TiO_2 光催化联合催化降解有机废水的新型深度氧化处理新技术——超声光催化技术。实验结果表明，尽管超声光催化反应对苯胺及其衍生物的降解协同效应并不是很显著，但是超声光催化反应对苯胺及其衍生物却具有较好的降解率，而且不同有机化合物结构对超声光催化反应有着较大的影响。

(2) 研究了泥炭生物滤塔处理含低浓度 H_2S 恶臭气体的技术。实验考察并研究了

气体停留时间和 H_2S 进气负荷对 H_2S 去除率的影响,生物滤塔的抗冲击负荷能力以及生物降解宏观动力学。结果表明,当停留时间为 25～30 s 时,进气质量浓度为 3～70 mg/m^3,去除率达到 99% 以上,且具有较强的抗冲击负荷。

请将下面两篇文摘翻译成中文:

(1) A group function, relation curve between flax (f) and bulk phase concentration of substrate (S) was set up. The biodegradation kinetic of organic compounds of acrylic fiber wastewater in biofilm is studied (the treatment technology is coagulation/sedimentation-anoxic/aerobic biofilm process), and the results showed that the concentration of non-degradation pollutants in effluent is 77 mg/L. In aerobic zone, the half-rate constant is 72.84 mg/L, the maximum removal rate of organic compounds at unit area filler is very low, 0.089 $g/(m^2 \cdot d)$, which corresponds to the fact chat there are some biorefractory compounds in the wastewater.

(2) The conventional "pump-and-treat" technology for subsurface remediation of groundwater contaminated with volatile organic compounds (VOCs), has limitation of prohibitively long treatment time due to extremely low water solubility of the VOCs. Surfactant-based soil remediation has emerged as the effective technology that substantially reduces the treatment time. In order to make the whole process economical, the surfactant used in soil washing has to be recovered and reused. This study examined the recovery of anionic surfactant, sodium dodecyl sulfate (SDS), from soil remediation fluids containing TCA, using a bench-scale membrane pervaporation unit. The effects of high TCA concentration, surfactant dosage, and flow rate on permeation flux and selectivity (a value) of the process were evaluated. In general, higher surfactant concentration yielded lower TCA flux and constant water flux, resulting in declining a values; higher flow rate of TCA feed stream results in higher VOC flux and selectivity, an indication of the effect of concentration polarization; higher TCA feed concentration produce higher TCA permeation across the membrane, however, the selectivity was virtually unchanged unless the total TCA concentration exceeded $2,000 \times 10^{-6}$.

Chapter 13　Scientific Paper

科技论文属于学术论文的范畴,它是论述科技领域中具有创新意义的理论性、实验性、观测性的新成果、新见解和新知识;或者是总结某种已知原理应用于实践所取得的新方法、新技术和新产品的科技文献。科技论文是反映科研成果、开展学术交流的重要手段,科技论文写作是科技工作者必备的一种技能。通过撰写科技论文,科技工作者可以将自己在从事科学研究或承担专门技术工作中所取得的成果展示给同行。

科技论文的类型多种多样,但对科技论文写作的共同要求一般是:

(1)作为一篇科技论文,必须要有重要的科学价值,要报道新数据、新方法、新观点,总之,要有创新。

(2)作者思路必须清晰,论述要合乎逻辑。例如研究这个问题的目的是什么?前人研究过这个问题吗?前人的研究有什么不完善之处?你有什么新的见解和发现?科学价值和应用前景如何?

(3)准确表达自己的观点,措辞要反复推敲。对于作者论文中所运用的事实、经验材料和理论,一定要真实可靠。

(4)论证要严密,要将整个研究置于客观事实的基础上,任何假设和推论都必须有客观的、科学的依据;正确运用分析和综合、演绎和归纳等基本科学方法,注意因果关系和逻辑上的连贯性与一致性。

(5)一定要实事求是,客观地评价前人和自己的成果,对于论文所得结论的前提、条件、适用范围等,都应交代清楚。

(6)叙述要完整,每一个论据都要有一个合乎逻辑的结论。

(7)写作要简练,要用尽可能少的词句把意思表达清楚。但论文也不能过于简略,以至于连同行也看不懂。

科技论文常常因所属学科、研究项目、研究过程、研究方法不同等方面的原因,可以有多种写作方式和体例结构。因此,很难罗列出一切科技论文共同遵循的体例章法。但对于环境工程方面的论文,最常见的格式为 Introduction→Materials and methods→Results and discussion。即先提出问题,然后进行实验,再对所得的结果进行各种处理,从中找出某些规律性的东西。有时,文章的结尾可用 Conclusion 进行条理化。这种写法比较符合人们认识客观事物的顺序,一目了然。

上面的这种写作顺序只是对常见的环境工程专业刊物而言,对于其他刊物并不一定适用,即使对环境工程专业刊物也有许多例外,关键是论文的中心和重心是什么,如何围绕中心展开自己的论文。

此外,一篇完整的论文还应有标题(Title)、作者(Author)、摘要(Abstract)、致谢(Acknowledgments)以及参考文献(References)等部分。

13.1　Title

科技论文的标题是其基本思想的浓缩与概括。一则好的标题应该确切、鲜明、扼要地概括论文的基本思想,使读者在未看论文的摘要和正文之前即能迅速、准确地判明论文的基本内容,从而作出是否阅读摘要和正文的判断。不恰当的标题往往会使真正需要阅读论文的读者错过阅读此篇论文的机会,从而使标题完全失去它应起的作用。我国科技期刊要求论文题名一般不超过20个汉字,外文题名一般不超过10个实词。

拟订标题时应该注意以下几方面的问题。

(1)标题常用的词类有名词、名词词组或名词短语,不要使用介词短语或不定式动词短语。一般不使用完整的句子,尽量做到简明扼要,但并非越简单越好,过于简单反而使标题笼统。例如下面两个标题:

E.g.1:Effects of some heavy metals complex contamination on soil microbial community.

一些重金属复合污染对土壤环境微生物群落的影响。

E.g.2:Effects of Cu, Zn, Cd and Pb complex contamination on soil microbial community.

重金属铜、锌、镉、铅复合污染对土壤环境微生物群落的影响。

第一个标题涉及面太笼统,没有指出研究的是哪几种重金属;而第二个标题就比第一个好,准确地反映了文章的研究内容,缩小了所研究的元素范围。

(2)对于研究性论文,也可以用描述性写法,将论文的性质、研究的内容乃至使用的手段等都说明清楚。例如下面这些标题:

E.g.1:Application of biosorption of surplus activated sludge in reducing the concentration of heavy metals in urban sewage sludge.

利用剩余活性污泥的生物吸附降低城市污水污泥重金属含量。

E.g.2:Catalytic Ozonation of Trace Nitrobenzene in Water by Iron Hydroxide.

水合氧化铁催化臭氧氧化去除水中痕量硝基苯。

E.g.3:Study on Odors Treatment by the Combination of Bacteria and Fungi.

细菌与真菌复合作用处理臭味气体的试验研究。

E. g. 4：Treatment of Sulfanilamide Production Waste Water by Resin Adsorption Technique.

树脂吸附法处理磺胺脒生产废水的工艺。

E. g. 5：Treatment of Nitrobenzene by Combining Electrolysis Reduction and Biodegradation.

电催化还原－生物降解耦合处理硝基苯废水。

（3）按惯例,英语标题字母大小写可以采用下面三种方法中的任何一种:第一种方法要求标题中每个词的每个字母都大写;第二种方法要求标题中第一个词的第一个字母和每个实词的第一个字母都大写;第三种方法只要求标题中第一个词的第一个字母大写。其中第二种方法使用最为普遍。例如下面这些标题:

E. g. 1：PHOTOCATALYTIC DEGRADATION OF ANILINE IN WATER ON IMMOBILIZED TITANIUMDIOXIDE.

负载型二氧化钛光催化降解苯胺。

E. g. 2：Preparation of Titanium Dioxide Particles and Properties for Flue Gas Desulfurization.

二氧化钛颗粒的制备及其对烟道气体的脱硫性能。

E. g. 3：The removal mechanisms of fluoride ion by aluminum salt coagulant.

铝盐混凝去除氟离子的作用机理探讨。

（4）如果一个标题太长,或者涵盖相互独立的内容太多,也可以使用副标题。副标题多半是对主标题的补充。例如下面这些标题:

E. g. 1：Comparing Biological Responses to Mill Process Changes：A Study of Steroid Concentrations in Goldfish Exposed to Effluent and Waste Streams from a Canadian Bleached Sulphite Mill.

生物响应和工厂生产过程的变化对比:加拿大漂白亚硫酸盐工厂的污水和废水沟中的金鱼体内类固醇浓度的研究。

E. g. 2：Removal of Natural Organic Matter by Ultrafiltration：Characterization, Fouling and Cleaning.

超滤法去除天然有机物质:特性、结污和清洗。

E. g. 3：Interactions Between Natural Organic Matter（NOM）and Membranes：Rejection and Fouling.

天然有机物质和膜之间的相互作用:排斥和结污。

E. g. 4：Detoxification of a Mixture of Aliphatic Chlorinated Hydrocarbons in a Fixed-Bed Bioreactor：Continuous On-line Monitoring via an Attenuated Total Reflection-Fourier Transform Infrared Sensor.

脂肪族氯化烃混合物在固定床生物反应器中的解毒作用:通过衰减全反射-傅立叶转换红外传感器连续在线检测。

E. g. 5：Nutrients Within Integrated Bleached Kraft Mills：Sources and Behavior in Aerated Stabilization Basins.

漂白牛皮纸联合厂的营养物的研究:来源及其在曝气稳定池中的性质。

(5)有的研究课题在相似的研究方法或条件下进行了一系列研究,这时可使用系列标题,即先确定一个长期不变的总标题,子标题标在总标题后面,前面标以序列号。一般说来,总标题比较概括,子标题直接表明研究的对象或结果。

E. g. 1：Photochemical decomposition of 2,4 - dichlorophenoxy acetic acid (2,4 - D) in aqueous solution I. kinetic study.

水溶液中2,4 - D 的光化学降解：I. 动力学研究。

Photochemical decomposition of 2,4 - dichlorophenoxy acetic acid(2,4 - D) in aqueous solution II. Reactor modeling and verification.

水溶液中2,4 - D 的光化学降解：II.反应器建模和验证。

E. g. 2：Identification and characterization of water quality transients using wavelet analysis I. wavelet analysis methodology.

通过微波分析鉴定和描述水质瞬变过程:I. 微波分析法。

Identification and characterization of water quality transients using wavelet analysis II. Application to electronic water quality data.

通过微波分析鉴定和描述水质瞬变过程:II. 在电子水质数据分析中的应用。

(6)要严格控制标题长度,例如美国数学学会要求投稿论文的标题长度不超过12个词。因此,标题长度多少为宜,最好在投稿前仔细阅读所投刊物的征稿简则(Instructions for Authors),按要求而定。

13.2　Author

科技论文既可以个人名义署名,也可以集体名义署名。如以个人名义署名,则应在论文题目后写明作者全名,并且另起一行写上作者的工作单位、国别、所在城市和邮政编码。自然科学研究往往由一个集体来完成,作者姓名很多,但必须标出一个通信联系人(Corresponding Author)。按中国人的习惯,姓写在前面,名字写在后面;而按英语国家的习惯,姓写在后,名字在前。因此,在向国外投稿时,可以根据对方的要求注明自己的名字和姓。下面是几个例子:

E. g. 1：

CHEN Yingxu, LIN Qi, LU Fang, HE Yunfeng

(Department of Environmental Science, Zhejiang University, Huajiachi, Hangzhou, 310029)

E.g.2:

I. Koyuncu F. yalcin and I. Ozturk

(ITU Civil Engineering Faculty, Environmental Engineering Department 80626, Maslak, Istanbul, Turkey)

E.g.3:

P. Jokela* and P. Keskitalo**

(*Institue of Water and Environmental Engineering, Tampere University of Technology. Korkeakoulunkatu 4, FIN-33720 Tampere, Finland**Tritonet Ltd, Pinninkatu 53C. FIN-33100 Tampere, Finland)

E.g.4:

CHENG Shu-pei, SHI Lei, ZHANG Xu-xiang, YAN Jun, DING Zhong-hai, HAO Chun-bo

(The National Key Laboratory of Pollution Control and Resource Reuse, Department of Environmental Sciences, Nanjing University, Nanjing 210093 China. E-mail chengsp@ nju.edu.cn)

E.g.5:

XU Ren-kou[1], ZHU Yong-guan[2]*, David Chittleborough[3]

(1. Institute of Soil Science, Chinese Academy of Sciences, Nanjing 210008, China; 2. Research Centre for Eco-Environmental Sciences, Chinese Academy of Sciences, Beijing 100085, China. E-mail: ygzhu@mail.rcees.ac.cn. 3. Soil and land system, school of earth and Environmental Sciences, The University of Adelaide, SA 5005, Australia)

13.3　Introduction

13.3.1　How to write an introduction

常言道:万事开头难。引言是论文的开场白,也是较难写的一部分。引言是表明作者讨论该论题的动机或目的及论题的范围和焦点,或者提出有待阐述的观点。一个良好的开头会为读者阅读论文提供导向,引导读者明确地领会此项科学成果的意义、目的、实验采用的方法和创新点。

撰写引言要开门见山,不绕圈子;言简意赅,突出重点;尊重科学,实事求是。引言不应与摘要重复,不应展开讨论。

常见的引言一般包含下列内容:

(1)本课题研究的内容;

(2)背景材料,即其他研究人员在该领域进行过哪些研究?现状如何?存在哪些问题?

(3)本研究的目的,即作者要解决什么问题;

(4)作者采用什么方法解决此问题?为何采用这一研究方法?同以前的研究有什么不同?

(5)作者的主要研究结果有哪些?

即在明确了作者的研究方向以后,通过背景材料,即介绍该领域的过去、现状及存在的问题,明确自己的课题与以往有哪些不同,从而确定作者的研究范围。

在介绍历史背景时重点应放在资料介绍上,应该引用在该领域有重要影响并与本研究直接相关的文献,将该领域中互不相同的各派观点或混淆的概念抽提出来,以表明作者熟悉此研究的有关情况,进而提出本文要研究的问题。

(6)下一步应说明深入研究有关问题的必要性,进一步说明研究目的。对某一问题进一步开展研究,原因可能是多方面的:以往的研究在某些方面尚未取得结果;以往的研究结果大相径庭;以往研究中提出的新问题需深入探讨等。在说明课题研究意义时,经常使用的词是"could""may""should"等。

(7)对于作者采用的研究方法,应说明为什么所采用的研究方法特别适用于此课题。

(8)最后要列举主要的研究结果,以促使读者读完全文,对研究结果作出评价。

Introduction 的写法没有统一的格式,长短也不一,视文章的内容和背景材料而定,下面是几个例子:

E.g.1: Estuaries, as the fertile marine ecosystems, are crucial to the life cycle of many aquatic organisms. However, rapid industrialization and urbanization in recent years have led to widespread contamination of heavy metals in the coastal and estuarine sediments, and impose direct threat or potential risk on the local ecosystem (Chapman, 2001). Therefore, detailed studies on the biological and ecological significance of metal contamination in sediments are urgently required. Since the acute and chronic impacts of heavy metals are usually dependent on the existing chemical forms rather than total concentrations, extra attention must be paid on metal speciation when evaluating the environmental implications (Forstner, 1993).

The hydrodynamic conditions in Deep Bay, a semi-enclosed bay, are different from the the adjacent Pearl River Estuary (PRE) in South China. In recent years, the local environment faces great pressure due to the increasing discharges of industrial effluents, domestic sewage and livestock wastewater via runoffs along the bank (Hills, 1998; Lau, 2000). The objective of the present study is to investigate the current distribution and associations of heavy metals in the overlying water, bottom sediments and suspended particles.

E. g. 2: The anaerobic ammonia oxidation (Anammox) is a novel biological reaction which produces molecular nitrogen with ammonia as electron donor and nitrite as electron acceptor, respectively (Van de Graff, 1996). Anammox process becomes a promising substitute to the conventional denitrifying process because it removes two pollutants (ammonia and nitrite) simultaneously at a low cost (Jetten, 1997). However, Anammox bacteria grow slowly and their cell yield is very small. In order to bring the process into practical use, some measures must be taken to get the inoculum for start-up of the bioreactor and to promote growth of Anammox bacteria (Strous, 1999; Zheng, 2001).

Some aerobic ammonia oxidizers show both metabolic diversity and substrate diversity. They oxidize ammonia not only under aerobic conditions but also under anaerobic conditions (Bock, 1995), and carry out denitrification with hydrogen or ammonia as electron donor (Van de Graff, 1996). The metabolic diversity and subatrate diversity of ammonia oxidizers lead us to a new strategy to solve the above-mentioned problems, that is, to start up Anammox bioreactor with nitrifying activated sludge. The feasibility of the start-up strategy is investigated in this paper.

E. g. 3: Deteriorating atmospheric air quality has resulted in more stringent regulations are being enforced to control air pollutants. Volatile organic compounds (VOCs) are among the new class of air contaminants generated from a variety of industrial sources. Efforts to control the emissions of VOCs have often failed due to inefficiency of conventional treatment systems such as wet scrubbing, ozonation, catalytic and thermal oxidation, and adsorption. Biotreatment of contaminants in gaseous streams provides an effective and inexpensive alternative to conventional treatment systems (Ottengraf, 1983; Leson, 1991; Deshusses, 1993). The possibility of complete mineralisation and effectiveness at low concentrations are other added advantages of biodegradation (Jorio, 1998; Sorial, 1997). Among the biological waste gas treatment methods, biofiltration is an innovative and a versatile, low technology approach to air pollution control which has attracted growing interest during the last few years (Ottengraf, 1983; Allen, 1991). A number of biomass supported on suitable matrices such as compost, peat, humus earth and wood chips have been used. The volatile compounds are adsorbed on the biofilm and subsequently oxidized into end products like water, carton dioxide and salts. Many experimental studies have established biofiltration as an efficient treatment process and reliable technology for the control of VOCs (Hodge, 1995; Shareefdeen, 1993; Tang, 1995; Corsi, 1995). The majority of the literatures on biofiltration are for removal of single compound. However, industrial emissions are generally mixtures of VOCs. In mixed culture systems with multiple substrates the biodegradation process may be completely different from pure substrate system due to complex interactions between the substrates and the microorganisms.

Ottengraf et al.'s (Ottengraf, 1983) investigating of the treatment of composite gas mixtures containing toluene, butyl acetate, ethyl acetate and butanol have reported that all the organic components were simultaneously eliminated with maximum elimination capacity for each compound ranging from $20-40$ g/(m^3 · h). Corsi and Seed (Corsi, 1995) treated a gas stream mixture containing 1:1:1 benzene, toluene and xylene in a compost media biofilter and reported an average removal efficiency of 95% for loading rates up to 2.8 kg COD m^3/d. Kiared et al. (Kiared, 1996) have reported high elimination capacities for both toluene and ethanol in laboratory scale biofilters treating a mixture of both.

Jorio et al. (Jorio, 1998) have extensively investigated the performance of the biofilter for the removal of high concentrations of toluene, xylene, and mixture of toluene and xylene. They achieved maximum elimination capacity of 115 g/(m^3 · h) for the mixture of toluene and xylene. They have reported that the metabolism of toluene degradation was inhibited by the presence of xylene in the mixture. This paper reports the results of study of biodegradation of a mixture of ethanol and methanol in a laboratory biofilter.

E.g.4: Granular sludge is a dense community made up of symbiotic organisms, possessing good biological activity and excellent mass transfer efficiency. There are millions of microorganisms per gram of biomass, which play different roles in removing biodegradable organic matter from municipal and industrial wastewater. Compared to conventional activated sludge, the aerobic granules have the advantages of dense and strong structure, good settling ability, and tolerance to high organic loading rates. Aerobic granulation would be applicable for improving treatment efficiency, renovating existing processes, and thus reducing construction and running cost.

Since 1990s, aerobic granular sludge has been cultivated successfully in aerobic upflow sludge blanket (AU.S.B) reactors (Mishima and Makamura, 1991; Shin et al., 1992). The factors influencing aerobic granulation were extensively studied, such as organic loading rate, settling time, hydrodynamic shear force and substrate composition (Beun et al., 1999; Chen et al., 2006; Iaconi et al., 2005, 2006; Jang et al., 2003; Li et al., 2006; Liu et al., 2005; Qin et al., 2004; Su and Yu, 2005; Sun et al., 2006; Tay et al., 2004; Wang et al., 2005; Zheng et al., 2005; Zhu and Wilderer, 2003; Zhai et al., 2006). However, the cultivation of aerobic granular sludge is a complicated ecological process, in which many factors need to be further investigated. Because detailed information of the temperature effects on aerobic granulation is limited, it becomes our research objective to reveal the granulation process and mechanisms under different temperatures.

In this article, aerobic granulation was achieved in three sequencing batch airlift reactors (SBAR). The morphology of granular sludge, their settling properties and treatment efficiencies under different temperatures were discussed. Polymerase chain reaction-denaturing gradient gel electrophoresis (PCR-DGGE) was employed for revealing the microbial community structure and succession corresponding to different temperatures. The aim of this study is to enrich the knowledge of cultivation mechanisms, and to accelerate the applied research of aerobic granular sludge in wastewater treatment.

E.g.5: Laccases (benzenediol: oxygen oxidoreductases, EC 1.10.3.2) be-long to the multicopper oxidases (MCOs) family that normally contain four copper atoms. These enzymes are of particular interest with regard to various industrial applications based on their ability to utilize a broad range of substrates (Dwivedi et al., 2011). Indus-trial processes are often carried out at harsh environment, such as high temperature, high salt concentration or extremely acidic or alkaline pH. Therefore, resistant laccases are required to maintain high activity under these adverse physicochemical conditions (Santhanam et al., 2011). Fungal laccases usually show high redox potential and production yield than bacterial laccases (Dwivedi et al., 2011; Uzan et al., 2010; Fan et al., 2011). However, the majority of fungal laccases suffer from the drawbacks of low thermostability, narrow pH range as well as susceptible to salts, which limited their practical application (Fang et al., 2012; Santhanam et al., 2011).

In recent years, rapid progress has been made in finding and application of prokaryotic laccase. Bacterial laccases have great potential as biocatalysts due to their intrinsic properties of high thermal and alkaline pH stability (Singh et al., 2011). The major obstacle for their commercial application is the lack of sufficient enzyme stocks, as the production yield from native sources is usually very low (Dubé et al., 2008b). Recombinant production of enzymes in easily cultivable and handling hosts is often one of the best choices to achieve higher productivity. The most common host for nheterologous protein expression is Escherichia coli, which is characterized for its fast growth and easy genetic manipulation (Banerjee et al., 2009). To date, several bacterial laccases have been successfully expressed in *E. coli* (Santhanam et al., 2011). However, all these recombinant enzymes were located intracellularly, which was difficult to purify and thus increased the production cost (Santhanam et al., 2011). Moreover, the recombinant laccase often formed insoluble aggregates, leading to significantly low yield (Martins et al., 2002; Suzuki et al., 2003; Fang et al., 2011). To solve these problems, extracellular protein expression may be an ideal alternative.

Pichia pastoris is one of the most effective expression systems for the secretion of recombinant proteins (Damasceno et al., 2012). It offers several advantageous features including ease of genetic manipulation and rapid growth rate like bacteria. Meanwhile, foreign proteins can be secreted into the culture medium, which avoids the intracellular accumulation of target protein and simplifies the purification steps (Damasceno et al., 2012). We have recently reported the characterization and decolorization ability of a novel spore-associated laccase from *Bacillus licheniformis* (Lu et al., 2012). The spore laccase was featured by its excellent tolerance towards high temperature, alkaline pH and chloride, which make it a promising candidate for dye decolorization in textile industry. However, it is difficult to obtain this enzyme in a robust and inexpensive way due to its spore-bound nature (Hullo et al., 2001; Martins et al., 2002). In this investigation, we have cloned the laccase gene of *B. licheniformis* to investigate its effective expression in *P. pastoris*. The recombinant enzyme was purified, characterized and tested for its ability in dye decolorization.

E. g. 6: Aerobic nitrifying granules have excellent settling ability, higher biomass retention, a strong capability to withstand shock loadings and high nitrogen removal capacity. Recently, some researchers have paid more attention to process parameters, operation mode, reactor types, and microbial community structure during aerobic nitrifying granules cultivation (Shi et al., 2010; Cydzik – Kwiatkowska and Wojnowska – Baryła, 2011; Shi et al., 2011; Wang et al., 2012; Yan et al., 2013; Li et al., 2010; Wu et al., 2012; Shen et al., 2013; Li et al., 2014), these studies indicate that aerobic nitrifying granular sludge has superior efficiency and lower consumption, so it would be regarded as a promising biological nitrogen removal technology, showing a broad application prospect in the field of wastewater treatment.

Although aerobic nitrifying granules have attracted considerable attention around the world, the relationship between the microbial population structure and performances has been still lack of in-depth discussion. The performances of aerobic denitrifying granular sludge fundamentally depend on their microbial population structure that is closely related to the seed sludge selected. Ma et al. and Song et al. have demonstrated the effect of microbial community on the properties of aerobic granules through culturing aerobic granules with seed sludge from different sources (Ma et al., 2010; Song et al., 2011), however, to date, little attention has been paid to the influence of microbial community structure of seed sludge on aerobic nitrifying granules.

In this paper, aerobic nitrifying granules were cultured in sequencing batch airlift reactors (SBAR) using activated sludge from domestic and beer wastewater treatment plant as seed sludge respectively, molecular biological technique was adopted to identify the microbial community structure of aerobic nitrifying granules, and the influence of microbial community on the physical and chemical properties of aerobic nitrifying granules was investigated, which would be expected to provide new basic information for directed acclimatization of aerobic nitrifying granular sludge.

13.3.2 Useful expressions and sentence patterns

as early as the 1970s	早在20世纪70年代
in the early 1970s	早在20世纪70年代
as far back as the 1970s	早在20世纪70年代
since 1970	自1970年以来
in recent years	近年来
in recent decades	近几十年来
during the last 30 years	近30年来

Chapter 13 Scientific Paper

in the subsequent years	随后几年
in the last decade	在过去的十年里
for this purpose	为此
There is current interest in...	……具有现实意义
...is of considerable current interest	……具有现实意义
With the development of...	随着……的发展
It is necessary to...	很有必要……
It is well documented that...	已经充分证明……
There is increasing evidence showing that...	越来越多证据显示……
There are no published data for...	……无报道
With respect to...	至于……
The former research mainly concentrated on...	以前的研究主要集中在……
...is a subject of much concern	……是很受关注的课题
...is a subject of current interest	……是具有现实意义的课题
...has been reported	……已报道
...has not been reported	……还没有报道
It has a broad application foreground in...	……具有广阔的应用前景
But little attention has been paid to...	很少关注……
Recent investigations showed that...	最近的研究表明……
The study of... has aroused great attention	对……的研究已引起人们的极大关注
It is well recognized that...	人们普遍认为……
Previous researches have showed that...	以前的研究表明……
However, few researches have been done to...	然而,……方面却很少有研究
The goal of our research is...	我们的研究目的是……
The main objective of this paper is...	本文的主要目的是……
The present study was to investigate...	本研究是为了探讨……
In order to solve this problem...	为了解决这个问题……
The present effort is an attempt to understand...	试图理解……
To achieve this goal...	为此目的……

13.4 Materials and Methods

本节主要介绍研究过程中使用的材料和方法。实验材料要做详细说明,应写明材料的确切技术规格、数量、来源及其制备方法,有时还应一一列出所使用试剂的化学性能和物理性能。介绍研究中使用的材料时应尽量采用各学科领域中的标准术语。如果在某国发表论文,就应该采用该国的标准术语。除由独家公司生产的独特产品外,一般产品使用其普通名称。

所用的实验仪器、设备,要标明使用条件、各种参数。

论文中应介绍研究中采用的方法,主要有三个方面的原因:首先,所用方法是读者评估课题质量的重要手段,如果研究程序有误,研究结果的可靠性就值得怀疑。因此,应以充分的理由说明所用方法既正确又可靠。其次,如果采用一种新方法,介绍研究方法的重要性更是不言而喻。最后,科学研究中有一条法则,凡采用同一方法,应可取得相同的结果。因此,为使他人能取得相同的结果,必须详细描述课题研究中采用的方法。

在介绍研究方法时,首先应说明采用该方法的前提是什么,需要做哪些准备工作。说明前提后,应按研究工作的逻辑顺序、不是实验的先后顺序来描述研究程序中的每个步骤,其中一些类似的步骤可合并介绍。有时用简明流程图或仪器草图说明会更好些。

与介绍使用的材料时一样,如果采用新的研究方法,当然应做详尽的描述和介绍。如果采用同行熟悉的方法,论文中只需做一般性介绍。如果其他常见文献对作者采用的研究方法做过详细介绍,则只需指出文献的名称与出处。

下面是几篇材料与方法部分的例文(以下例文为重点表述科技论文的写作方法,故涉及的图、表不在书中列出)。

E. g. 1: Materials and methods

1. Inoculum and basal medium

The aerobic activated sludge from Hangzhou Shibao Sewage Plant served as inoculum for Anammox bioreactor. Some physical and chemical properties are as follows: total suspended solid (TSS) 39.87 g/L, volatile suspended solid (VSS) 15.6 g/L, VSS/TSS 39.13%、pH 6.94.

The basal medium used in the experiment contained (per liter of water): KH_2PO_4(0.027 g), $MgSO_4 \cdot H_2O$(0.300 g), $CaCl_2$(0.136 g), $KHCO_3$(0.500 g), and 1 ml/L of trace element solution I and II. Trace element solution I contained (per liter of water): EDTA 5.000 g, $FeSO_4$ 5.000 g. Trace element solution II contained (per liter of water) EDTA 15.000 g, H_3BO_4 0.014 g, $ZnSO_4 \cdot 7H_2O$ 0.430 g, $MnCl_2 \cdot 4H_2O$ 0.990 g, $CuSO_4 \cdot 5H_2O$ 0.250 g, $NaMoO_4 \cdot 2H_2O$ 0.220 g, $NiCl_2$ 0.199 g, $NaSeO_4 \cdot 10H_2O$ 0.210 g.

2. Reactor system

The laboratory-scale bioreactor was made of grass with working volume of 1.3 L, height of 0.65 m and internal diameter of 0.10 m. Soft padding was filled for bacteria to grow. Three sampling ports were evenly distributed on the reactor. The flow diagram of the reactor system is shown in Figure 13.1.

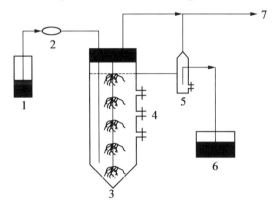

Figure 13.1 The Anammox bioreactor system and its diagram

1—influent tank—2. pump;3. reactor;4—sampling port;
5—gas-liquid-solid separator;6—effluent tank;7—gas out

The influent was pumped into the bottom of the reactor and flowed upward through the biofilm. The treated effluent passed the gas-liquid-solid separator and was then collected in the effluent bottle. The nitrogen gas was led off by gas-tube. The bioreactor was covered with a black cloth to eliminate the inhibition of light on Anammox activity.

3. Analyses

The concentration of NH_4^+-N, NO_2-N, NO_3-N were determined using the standard method issued by the Environmental Protection Agency (EPA) of China. The pH was determined using glass electrodes connected to pHS-9V pH-meter. Dissolved oxygen concentration was determined using YSI MODEL58 DO-meter. The most probable number (MPN) of nitrifying bacteria was determined as described by Chen (Chen, 1998). TSS was determined by drying the sample at 105 °C for at least 24 h. After burned at 550 °C for 1 h, the ash was measured. The difference between TSS and ash was termed VSS.

E. g. 2: Materials and methods

1. Filter materials

The packing material for the bed consisted of a mixture (60:40 v/v) of sieved compost (4 mm and 10 mm size granules, 1:1 ratio) and polystyrene inert particles (4 mm size). The inert material severed to increase the bed porosity and in ensure a more homogenous gas distribution across the filter bed. The filter material was inoculated with methanol and ethanol acclimated mixed microorganisms.

2. Organisms and culture medium

A mixed culture of microorganisms obtained from an activated sludge plant treatment and acclimated to a mixture of ethanol and methanol as the carbon source was used as an inoculum. The nutrient solution consisted of (g/L): $K_2HPO_4 - 0.8$, $KH_2PO_4 - 0.2$, $CaSO_4 - 0.05$, $MgSO_4 \cdot 7H_2O - 0.5$, $(NH_4)_2SO_4 - 1.0$ and $FeSO_4 \cdot 7H_2O - 0.01$ in water.

3. Experimental set-up

Figure 13.1 (omitted) illustrates the schematic diagram of the experimental set up. The biofilter made of transparent polyacrylic tube with an internal diameter of 5 cm. The tube was packed to a height of 50 cm. The filter material was supported by perforated plate. Sampling pods covered with rubber septa allowed collection of samples for analysis. A mixture of ethanol and methanol in humidified air was prepared from air streams of individual solvents in a glass-mixing chamber. The composition of the mixture was controlled by controlling the airflow rates using rotameter.

4. Biodegradation of mixtures

The biodegradation of mixtures of methanol and ethanol in the biofilters was studied at various proportions (20% – 80%). The biomass was acclimatized to a mixture concentration of 2 g/m^3 (50:50) at a flow rate 0.012 m^3/h. After steady state removal was achieved, the biofilter was operated at different initial concentrations, at different flow metes (0.012 – 0.024 m^3/h). Experiments were ran over a period of 70 – 80 hours. Effluent gas samples were collected at regular intervals and analyzed for residual ethanol and methanol concentrations.

5. Analytical methods

Ethanol and methanol were analyzed by gas chromatography (NUCON-5765, GC India) using a chromosorb-101 SS parked column (20 mm diameter x 3 m length) and a flame ionization detector. Nitrogen was used as the carries gas. The temperatures of the column, injector and detector were maintained at 150 ℃, 160 ℃ and 165 ℃ respectively.

E. g. 3: Materials and methods

1. Reagent

Atrazine (99%) was purchased from Chemical Service Company of U. S.. All the other reagents were A. R.

2. Soil

Soil tested was sampled from the farm of Zhejiang University. Some physical and chemical properties of the soil are listed in Table 1.

3. Experimental design

Activities of urease, invertin, acid phosphatase and catalase were selected as indexes and acid rain, Cu^{2+}, atrazine and incubation time as factors. The factor of acid rain was decomposed as H^+ and Al^{3+} according to the theory of soil acidity. The factors and levels are shown in Table 2. Atrazine is a typical contamination and H^+, Cu^{2+} influence the activity of hydrolase significantly. After the analysis of each factor they were listed again for an orthogonal table in order to study the interactions of acid rain, heavy metal and pesticide.

The air-dry soil were sieved (1 mm) and mixed with all contaminations shown in Table 2 in flasks with enough shaking. The H^+ was mixed by sulfuric acid and nitric acid (5:1) and Al^{3+}, Cu^{2+} were added as aluminum sulfate and cupric sulfate. Water was added till 80% of the maximum water capacity of soil. The reaction mixture was incubated at 28 ℃ in dark, constant temperature and moisture place. Three duplicate samples were utilized contrasting with control tests.

4. Measurement method

Activities of urease and acid phophatase were measured by colorimetric method and invertase and catalase, titrimetric method.

E. g. 4: Materials and methods

1. Reactor and operation

The laboratory-scale SBAR was used in this study with a working volume of 5.0 L, height-diameter ratio of 15:1, and volume commutative law of 50%. The gas flow in the surface was controlled at the speed of 2.4 m/s, aeration rate, organic load and running temperature were maintained at 0.24 m^3/h, 3.0 kg COD/m^3 · d and 30 ℃ respectively. The reactors were operated at a cycle of 6 h, including 5 min of influent filling, 5 min of effluent discharge, 20 min in the initial first cultivation stage to 3 min in the granules mature stage of settling, the rest time of aeration. The organic load was maintained constantly, the concentration of ammonia nitrogen of influent was increased from 80 mg/L to 140 mg/L, 200 mg/L and 260 mg/L gradually.

2. Synthetic wastewater

The main components of synthetic wastewater were as follows: $C_6H_{12}O_6$ · H_2O of 1,500 mg/L, NH_4Cl of 300 mg/L, $FeSO_4$ · $7H_2O$ of 30 mg/L, $MgSO_4$ · $7H_2O$ of 22.5 mg/L, $CaCl_2$ of 150 mg/L, K_2HPO_4 of 52.5 mg/L, KH_2PO_4 of 22.5 mg/L, beef extract of 75 mg/L, peptone of 112.5 mg/L, microelement of 1 mL/L. All chemicals used in this work were of analytical grade and used as received without further purification.

3. Seed sludge

Seed sludge was activated sludge obtained from sedimentation tank of Songjiang Beer Wastewater Treatment Plant and secondary sedimentation tank of Wenchang Municipal Sewage Treatment Plant, Harbin, China. The physico-chemical properties of the two kinds of seeding inoculum were shown in Table 1. The two reactors inoculated with different seed sludge were marked as R1 and R2 respectively.

The dominant bacterial groups in seed sludge taken from beer wastewater treatment plant were *Bacterium* PFCr-1, *Lysobacter ximonensis*, *Sphingobium vulgare*, *Clos-*

tridium bifermentans, and a kind of Estrogen-degrading bacterium. The dominant bacterial groups in inoculated sludge taken from municipal wastewater treatment plant were *Enterobacter* sp. , *Bacterium* PFCr-1, *Sphingomonas* sp. .

4. Analytical methods

The chemical oxygen demand (COD), NH_4^+-N, NO_2^--N, NO_3^--N, TN, SVI were measured using standard methods (State Environmental Protection Administration, 2002). Microorganisms were observed using an electronic microscope. Zeta potential was determined using micro-electrophoresis apparatus (JS94H). The specific oxygen uptake rate (SOUR) was measured according to Tong's method (Tong, 2010). The EPS was extracted using heat treatment method (Ni, 2012). The content of polysaccharide (PS) and proteins (PN) were measured using sulfuric acid-anthrone method (Mao et al. , 2012) and coomassie brilliant blue method (Wang et al. , 2012) respectively. Microbial community structure was analyzed using 16S rDNA molecular biological technique.

E. g. 5: Materials and methods

1. Materials

2, 2'-Azino-bis (3-ethylbenzothiaz oline-6-sulfonate) (ABTS), syringaldazine (SGZ), 2,6-dimethoxyphenol (2,6-DMP), reactive blue 19, reactive black 5, indigo carmine and acetosyringone were all Sigma-Aldrich products (St. Louis, MO, USA). Bacteria DNA Kit, Gel Extraction Kit and Plasmid Mini Kit I were purchased from Omega Bio-Tek (Norcross, GA, USA). Ex TaqDNA polymerase, T4 DNA ligase, primers, pMD18 – T plasmid and restriction enzymes were obtained from TaKaRa (Dalian, China). PageRuler prestained protein ladder was purchased from Fermentas (Ontario, Canada). Zeocin and expression vector pPICZ α A were purchased from Invitrogen (Carlsbad, CA, USA). Other chemicals were of analytical regent grade.

2. Microbial strains and media

B. *licheniformis* LS04 was isolated from forest soil (Lu et al. , 2012), and was deposited in China General Microbiological Culture Collection Center (CGMCC No. 4263). It was grown overnight in Luria-Bertani (LB) medium at 37 ℃ and 200 r. p.

m.. E. coli Top 10 competent cells (Tiangen, Beijing, China) were used for subcloning procedures and were grown in Low Salt LB medium. P. pastoris SMD1168H was products of Invitrogen (Carlsbad, CA, USA). Yeast extract-peptone-dextrose (YPD), buffered glycerol-complex (BMGY) and buffered minimal methanol (BMM) media were pre-pared according to the manual of the EasySelect Pichia Expression Kit (Invitrogen).

3. Cloning of laccase gene and homology modeling

Genomic DNA of B. licheniformis LS04 was prepared using the Bacteria DNA Kit. Amplification of the laccase gene was performed by PCR with forward primer 5'–CCGGAATTCAAACTTGAAAAATTCGTTG–3'and reverse primer 5'–CGGGGTACCT-TATTGATGACGAA–CATCTG–3'. Recognition sites of EcoRI and Kpn I are indicated by underline. The PCR amplication program was initiated at 94 ℃ for 4 min, followed by 30 cycles of 94 ℃ for 45 s, 53 ℃ for 45 s and 72 ℃ for 2 min, and a final extension at 72 ℃ for 10 min. The amplified DNA fragment was purified using Gel Extraction Kit, and was cloned into pMD18 – T vector. The recombinant pMD18 – T vector containing the laccase gene was digested with EcoRI and Kpn I and then ligated between corresponding sites of the digested pPICZ a A vector. The ligation mixture was transformed into E. coli Top10, and transformants were selected on Low Salt LB medium supplemented with 25l g/mL Zeocin. A map of the recom-binant plasmid pPICZ a A/lac as confirmed by sequence analysis is shown in Supplementary data Figure S1. Homology modeling of the B. licheniformis LS04 laccase was per-formed using the SWISS-MODEL server (http://swissmodel.exp-asy.org/) based on the template of Bacillus subtilis CotA protein (PDB ID: 1W8E).

4. Expression and purification of recombinant laccase

The pPICZ a A/lac vector was linearized with Sacl, and trans – formed into competent cells of P. pastoris by electroporation (Eppendorf Eporator, Humburg, Germany) at 1.5 kV with a 0.2-cm cuvette. Positive clones were selected on YPD plates supple-mented with 100 μg/mL Zeocin, and then transferred to BMM plates containing 0.5 mM ABTS and 0.1 mM $CuSO_4$. The BMM plates were incubated at 28 ℃ and 100 μL of methanol was added to the lid each day. Laccase-producing transformants were identi-fied by the presence of a dark green halo around the Pichia colonies.

Transformants with high laccase activity was inoculated in 25 mL BMGY medium, and incubated at 30 ℃, 200 r.p.m.. The cells were harvested by centrifugation at 3,000 g, 4 ℃ for 5 min when the OD_{600} of the culture reached 2.0 – 6.0. The cell pellets were resuspended in BMM medium containing 0.1 mM $CuSO_4$ to an OD_{600} of about 1.0. The flasks were cultivated at 30 ℃, 200 r.p.m., with 0.5% (v/v, final concentration) of methanol being added daily. Aliquots of culture supernatant were sampled every day to measure the enzyme activity. The supernatant was collected after 5 days by centrifugation at 3,000 g, 4 ℃ for 5 min. Purification of the recombinant laccase was performed using ultrafiltration, an-ion-exchange chromatography, and gel filtration according to Lu et al. (2007). Proteins were eluted with 20 mM sodium phosphate buffer (pH 7.5).

5. Enzyme assay

Laccase activity was measured at 30 ℃ using ABTS, syringaldazine (SGZ) and 2,6 – dimethoxyphenol (2,6 – DMP) as substrates (Lu et al., 2012). One unit of enzyme activity was defined as the amount of enzyme required to oxidize 1 μmol of substrate perminute. Protein concentration was determined using the Bradford Protein Assay Kit (Tiangen, Beijing, China) with bovine serum albumin as the standard. All assays were carried out in triplicate.

6. Characterization of the recombinant laccase

The molecular weight of the purified protein was determined by SDS-PAGE and gel filtration. SDS-PAGE was carried out using 12% polyacrylamide and stained with Coomassie Brilliant Blue R-250. Gel filtration was performed by Sephadex G-75 column calibrated with protein standard mixture containing lysozyme (14 kDa), chymotrypsinogen A (25 kDa), ovalbumin (43 kDa) and albumin (66 kDa). Deglycosylation of the purified laccase was performed using PNGase F (New England Biolabs, Ipswich, MA) according to the supplier's instructions. Zymography analysis for laccase activity was performed by separating unheated protein sample on 12% SDS polyacrylamide gel. The gel was washed with 0.1 M cit-rate-phosphate buffer (pH 4.0) for 5 min after electrophoresis. Protein bands with laccase activity were then visualized by immersing the gel in the same buffer containing 1 mM ABTS.

The effects of pH on laccase activity towards ABTS, SGZ and 2,6 – DMP were determined in 0.1 M citrate-phosphate buffer (pH 3.0 – 7.0) and 0.1 M Tris – HCl buffer (pH 7.0 – 9.0). The enzyme stability against pH was assayed by measuring the residual activity after incubation at 30 ℃ in pH 3.0, 7.0 and 9.0. The temperature optimum was recorded between 20 ℃ and 90 ℃ by following SGZ oxidation at pH 6.2. Thermostability was measured at 50 – 80 ℃ by incubating the enzyme in 20 mM citrate-phosphate buffer (pH 7.5). The residual laccase activity was determined using SGZ as the substrate. Kinetic parameters for the spore laccase (Lu et al., 2012) and purified laccase were determined at 30 ℃ using different concentrations of ABTS (10 – 1,000 μM), SGZ (5 – 100 μM), 2,6 – DMP (50 – 2,000 μM). The effects of inhibitors and organic solvents on enzyme activity were studied by determining the relative activity of the mixture with SGZ as the substrate. All assays were carried out in triplicate.

7. Dye decolorization

Decolorization of structurally different dyes by the purified laccase were carried out using reactive blue 19 (k_{max} = 591 nm), reactive black 5 (k_{max} = 597 nm) and indigo carmine (k_{max} = 610 nm). The reaction mixture (6 mL) contained 0.1 M citrate-phosphate buffer (pH 6.2) or 0.1 M Tris – HCl buffer (pH 9.0), dye (final concentration 100, 40 and 25 mg/L for reactive blue 19, reactive black 5 and indigo carmine, respectively), purified laccase (20 U/L) and acetosyringone (0.1 mM). Reactions were initiated by the addition of laccase, and incubated at 40 ℃ under mild shaking conditions. Control samples were run in parallel without laccase. All reactions were performed in triplicate.

13.5 Results and Discussion

13.5.1 Results and discussion writing

结果与讨论部分是文章的核心,最能体现论文质量的高低。对于初次写文章的人来说,这是最难写的一部分。这一部分除了给出作者的研究结果,还要对研究结果做出合理的解释,通过分析数据,找出内在的联系。此外,还要说明本研究结果与以往研究工作中一致和不一致的地方、本研究工作的局限性,并加以分析;对于此研究结果在理论和实践上的意义、应如何应用这些研究结果也要加以说明。

研究结果是论文的关键,它对作者和读者都很重要。论文中的所有推论均以此为根据,所以应对研究结果予以充分说明。如果某课题没有产生很多数据,研究结果主要通过描述性的句子来陈述;如果有很多数据,可以先做一概括性的介绍,然后列出有代表性的数据。如果需要列出大量的数据,那么使用图表更能反映出各种变化规律,使读者对论文的内容一目了然。图表可以是曲线图、流程图、照片、表格等。在图表的后面,作者可以用文字加以解释。

在写法上,最常见的是将 Results 与 Discussion 合起来写,图文并茂,边叙边议,大标题下还可以再细分成几个小标题,也可不加以细分直叙下去,讨论所得结果的变化趋势,总结各种规律,最后得出结论。当然,若两部分的内容相对独立,也可以分开来写。无论采用什么表现形式,以说明问题为主。

由于不同的论文其内容存在很大差异,因此结果与讨论没有固定的写法,作者只能根据自己的实验结果进行有针对性的讨论,下面是几个例子(以下例文为重点表述科技论文的写作方法,故涉及的图、表不在书中列出)。

E. g. 1: Results and discussion

1. Enrichment of nitrifying bacteria

The bioreactor was inoculated with 0.7 L of the aerobic activated sludge and was operated at 30 ℃. In order to enrich nitrifying bacteria, it was run under aerobic conditions far the first 51 d. Oxygen was supplied by an aeration pump at about 6.4 L/min and dissolved oxygen concentration was kept at about 6.5 mg/L. Influent solution was made by adding $(NH_4)_2SO_4$ into the basal medium and its pH value was adjusted to 7−8 with 0.5 mol/L $NaHCO_3$. Hydraulic retention time (HRT) was kept at 1 d, and influent ammonia concentration was raised step by step until 57 mmol/L was reached.

As shown in Figure 2, the performance of the bioreactor was not good with average ammonia removal of 74.79% during the first several days. From day 6 on, its performance improved. Effluent ammonia concentrations went down and then remained at a low level, while effluent nitrite and nitrate concentration gradually went up. On day 51, volumetric ammonia loading rate reached 56.96 mmol/(L·d), and volumetric conversion rate reached 56.85 mmol/(L·d). This implied that the activity of nitrifying sludge was gradually increased.

The results of bacteria counting experiment could give an explanation to the above-mentioned phenomenon. During the same period, the nitrifying bacteria grew quickly. On day 51, their number in the enriched sludge was almost 100 times higher than that in the seeding sludge (Table 1).

2. Start-up of anammox

When enough nitrifying bacteria were accumulated, the aeration pump was turned off. The bioreactor was sealed by a rubber stopper and was flushed with argon to remove dissolved oxygen. It was then fed with synthetic wastewater (5 mmol/L NH_4^+, 5 mmol/L NO_2^-). After ammonia and nitrite removal was higher than 90%, influent concentration was raised to 20 mmol/L by a step of 3 mmol/L over a period of 31 days, while HRT was kept at 1 d.

As shows in Figure 3, the bioreactor did not work well with average ammonia and nitrite removal as low as 34.79% and 61.04%, respectively. From day 10 on, its performance improved obviously. During the following 20 days, influent ammonia concentration was increased from 4.72 to 19.45 mmol/L and nitrite concentration from 5.02 to 19.82 mmol/L, progressively, both ammonia and nitrite removal were more than 90%. This indicated that Anammox bioreactor had been started up successfully.

It has been proved that there is a relation between aerobic ammonia oxidizers and anaerobic ammonia oxidizers. Anammox bacteria show many common physiological characteristics to nitrifiers. For example, they metabolize ammonia and hydroxylamine aerobically and their conversion product is nitrite (Zheng, 2000; 2001). On the contrary, some nitrifiers have Anammox activity, and can oxidize ammonia with nitrite as electron acceptor under strictly anaerobic condition (Strous, 1997). Moreover, a lot of nitrifiers have been detected in Anammox sludge (Van de Craff, 1996). The metabolic diversity of ammonia oxidizers offers a possibility for us to take nitrifying activated sludge as seeding sludge of Anammox bioreactor. This experiment has demonstrated that it is feasible to start up Anammox bioreactor with the enriched nitrifying sludge.

Ammonia oxidizers such as Nitrosomonas species show substrate diversity as well as metabolic diversity. They are able to carry out denitrification with either ammonia or hydrogen as electron donor (Van de Graff, 1996). The maximum growth rate of the former (0.96 – 1.92/d) is far higher than that of the latter (0.06/d) (Zheng, 1998; 2000; Strous, 1999). In theory, the substrate diversity of ammonia oxidizers offers another possibility for us to facilitate the growth of nitrifying activated sludge and to shorten the start-up period. The feasibility is under investigation (Figure 4).

E. g. 2: Results and discussion

1. Start up and acclimation

Acclimation is an important operation for the successful performance of biofilter. Biofilter was first acclimated 50:50 mixture of ethanol and methanol continuously at a flow rate of 0.012 m^3/h and a total concentration of 2.0 g/m^3. When microorganisms were acclimated to the mixture, a steady state was achieved in about 30 d with a visible biofilm growth and high removals of ethanol and methanol.

2. Biodegradation of mixtures

The biodegradation pattern of mixtures methanol and ethanol at three different proportions, 20:80, 50:50 and 80:20 are shown in Figures 2, 3, 4. It was observed that the removal efficiencies for both ethanol and methanol in the mixtures were much less than for the individual substrate. Even a low proportion of methanol (20%) in the mixture inhibited the degradation of readily biodegradable ethanol.

The presence of ethanol also decreased the removal of methanol. These inhibitory effects were more clearly seen with equal proportions of methanol and ethanol. In this case, the ethanol removal was inhibited by about 30% while the methanol removal was reduced from 40% to 8%. At higher proportion of methanol (80% in the mixture) the effect of ethanol on methanol degradation was highly significant while the inhibitory effect of methanol on the ethanol removal is not very evident. It is well recognized that in the case of biodegradation of two or more pollutants the metabolic activity may involve the mechanism of induction, inhibition or co-metabolism, depending on the substrates and microbial species present. Though, some evidences of such metabolic effects are reported in mixtures in liquid phase cultures, there are very few reports in biofiltration of mixtures.

Arvin et al. (Arvin, 1989) observed stimulation of biodegradation of benzene in liquid phase by the presence of either toluene or xylene. Chang et. al (Chang, 1993) found mutual inhibition in the biodegradation of a mixture of toluene and xylene in a suspension. In biofiltration, Deshusses and Hamer (Deshusses, 1993) observed inhibition of methyl isobutyl ketone (MIBK) biodegradation in the presence of methyl ethyl ketone (MEK). Interestingly, so far no explanation other than a competitive inhibition has been offered for the cross interactions between pollutants in multi polutant biodegradation.

The observation with mixtures in the present study may be explained in terms of two different groups of microorganisms namely ethanol utilizers and methanol utilizers, while the methanol utilizers have the ability to switch to ethanol utilization in the presence of ethanol, the ethanol utilizers seems to be inhibited by the presence of methanol. Thus, the lesser removal of methanol in the presence of ethanol appears to be due to preferential utilization of ethanol by the methanol degraders. The decrease in the ethanol removal in the presence of methanol seems to be related to the inhibitory effect of ethanol metabolism. However, more detailed microbiological studies are required to establish this differentiation in the biomass.

E. g. 3: Results and Discussion

Table 1 shows the viscosities (η) of the solutions in both neat DMAC and DMAC containing various additives. The addition of $CaCl_2$ to PAN/DMAC solution causes a decrease in η, and the viscosity is lowest (651 mPa/s) when $CaCl_2$ concentration is 2 wt. %. This indicates that the $CaCl_2$ as additive would increase the diffusion rate between solvent and nonsolvent (Shinde, 1999). Reuvers (Reuvers, 1987) designated instantaneous and delayed demixing as a cause of porous and dense skin membranes respectively. Instantaneous demixing should have a quick exchange rate of solvent and non-solvent, and delayed demixing have a slow rate. Some researchers have attempted to control the membrane morphology by adjusting the exchange rate of solvent and non-solvent (Cabasso, 1976; 1977).

The effect of the concentration of $CaCl_2$ in the casting solution on the flux of the resulting membranes could clearly be observed with a series of PAN membranes prepared under identical conditions (Table 1). It is clear from the data shown in Table 1 that an increase in the concentration of $CaCl_2$ in the casting solution leads to an increase in membrane pure water flux and the pure water permeability rate increases almost linearly. When the concentration of $CaCl_2$ is 3 wt%, the pure water flux of PAN membrane is 681 $L/(m^2 \cdot h)$ and, all of PAN membranes prepared from $CaCl_2$ have considerably higher flux than membranes prepared from neat DMAC.

The molecular weight cut off (MWCO) profiles are constructed for PAN membranes by measuring solute separation for four proteins of molecular weight ranging from 14,400 to 67,000 Dalton. For the various membranes prepared from

$CaCl_2$, as additive, the molecular weight cut off (MWCO) profiles (Figure 1) are superposed at molecular weight of protein higher than 35,000 Dalton and the molecular weight cut off is found to be around 60,000 Dalton. The results indicated that $CaCl_2$ as additive can increase the pure water flux of PAN membrane and does not change the average pore size significantly compared with the PAN membrane prepared without any additive in the casting solution. Shinde et al. (Shinde, 1999) reached the same conclusion by examining the effect of various inorganic halides (LiCl, $ZnCl_2$ and $AlCl_3$) added to a casting solution of PAN in N, N – dimethyl formamide (DMF).

E. g. 4: Results and discussion

1. The morphology and physico-chemical properties of nitrifying granules

The variation of morphology (as shown in Figure 1) was observed regularly using Leica electronic microscope in the operational process of the reactors.

As shown in Figure 1, a large amount of flocculent sludge presented predominantly in both R1 and R2 after 8 days cultivation, kernel in some particles existed clearly in R1, the color of sludge changed from dark grayish-black before inoculation to shallow grey gradually, meanwhile, the SVI value of the sludge was maintained at 50 – 60 mL/g, showing better settling ability. After 42 days continuous running, the floc reduced gradually, and a large number of granular sludge with clear outline emerged in R1 and R2, SVI decreased to 30 – 40 mL/g around. After 85 days, the granular sludge in R1 and R2 had become mature with compact structure and smooth surface, the granules in R1 were rounded, smooth and dense, the size of which was larger as revealed in Figure 1(c) than in Figure 1(f), the granular sludge in R1 and R2 had good settling capacity with SVI value of 21.39 mL/g and 23.87 mL/g respectively.

In the process of aerobic nitrifying granules cultivation, SOUR, Zeta potential, EPS content and PN/PS ratio of granules were monitored regularly, the results were demonstrated in Table 2.

The content of SOUR, Zeta, EPS in granules increased significantly along with the augmentation of the microbial synergy metabolism during aerobic nitrifying granules cultivation (as shown in Table 2). At the initial stage of inoculation, the SOUR value in two reactors were both below 0.3 mgO_2/gMLVSS · min, which were increasing gradually as the reactors running, the SOUR value of mature granules in

R1 and R2 could reach 1.138 – 1.203 mgO$_2$/gMLVSS · min and 1.027 – 1.103 mgO$_2$/gMLVSS · min respectively. The seed sludge in R1 was activated sludge obtained from beer wastewater treatment plant, in which the microbial activity was relatively higher and has been maintained steady increase in the cultivating process with stable organics removal efficiency and no drastic fluctuations. As the increasing of microbial aerobic rate, the COD removal rate and NH_4^+-N removal rate were also high and stable, which could reach more than 90%. The Zeta potential value of granules in R1 increased significantly, while the Zeta potential value of granules in R2 presented fluctuating increase. After 60 – 110 days of cultivation, the Zeta potential in R1 was stable around – 4.0 mV, which reached nearly four times as much as that of seed sludge, indicating that the granules had become mature. Zeta potential of granules in R2 was still slow rise of fluctuations, and finally tends to be stable at 5.049 – 5.799 mV. The Zeta potential of aerobic nitrifying granules in R1 was higher than that in R2, and there was no drastic fluctuation, indicating that the hydrophobicity of granular sludge was good. The sludge hydrophobic hypothesis expounds that high hydrophobicity is conducive to the formation of granular sludge, and the better granules hydrophobicity is, the better granules stability is (Cheng et al., 2012).

The variation trends of EPS and PN/PS ratio in R1 and R2 were roughly similar, which was increasing slowly in the running process. The EPS content of seed sludge could reach 90.64 mg/g · VSS that was higher than that of 55.85 mg/g · VSS in R2. From 30th day to 60th day was the granules formation phase, in which the sharp increase of the EPS content presented the linear increase with the value of 163.93 mg/g · VSS and 143.27 mg/g · VSS respectively, the PN/PS ratio increased from 0.634 and 0.683 in seed sludge to 1.434 and 1.826 in R1 and R2 respectively. After 70 days of cultivation, the granules become mature, EPS content was stable at 178 mg/g · VSS and 160 mg/g · VSS respectively, the PN/PS ratio increased to 1.916 and 1.884 respectively. Previous studies have indicated that PN/PS ratio is closely related to the granulation degree (Seviour et al., 2012). The increase of PN/PS ratio in EPS could contribute to the decrease of negative charge, the increase of hydrophobicity in the sludge surface, the sludge flocculation and the stability of their structures (Liao et al., 2008).

The EPS derived from aerobic nitrifying granules is significantly influenced by microbial community structure, the cultured aerobic denitrifying granular sludge can secrete more EPS due to many polymer producing bacteria groups included in the seed sludge, which play an important role in keeping stabilization and hydrophobicity of granules.

2. Nitrogen removal characteristics of aerobic nitrifying granules

The NH_4^+-N values of influent and effluent of the reactors were monitored regularly in the running process, the results were illustrated in Figure 2.

As shown in Figure 2, the initial NH_4^+-N concentration was 80 mg/L, in the early running days of the reactors, the removal rate of NH_4^+-N was between 50% – 70% in both R1 and R2. With the formation of granular sludge, the removal efficiency gradually improved, the removal rate of NH_4^+-N could reach 91.59% and 79.78% respectively in R1 and R2 after 32 days running. Beginning from 36th day, the removal rate of NH_4^+-N in the reactors had a sharp decrease to 70.34% and 64.07% respectively, because the influent NH_4^+-N concentration was improved to 160 mg/L. Soon afterwards, the removal rate of NH_4^+-N increased gradually due to accommodation of various microbes, which were back to 89.50% and 79.22%. From 59th day of running, the concentration of NH_4^+-N was increased to 200 mg/L, in the first cycle after the increase, removal rate of NH_4^+-N was in a slight drop, then back soon, and have remained stable as the running of R1 and R2, indicating that the granules in the reactors have the stronger ability to resist impact. Running to 96th day, concentration of NH_4^+-N was improved to 260 mg/L to strengthen the nitrogen load capacity of the granular sludge. During the 96 – 108 days of running, the removal rate of NH_4^+-N in two reactors were in stable state, which could reach 89.42% and 75.69% respectively. According to the comparison, aerobic nitrifying granules in R1 have better nitrogen removal ability.

On the one hand, granules with superior performance in R1 may be intercepted down due to good sedimentation performance of granular sludge, which can prolong the sludge retention time inside the system and benefit the growth of nitrifying bacteria. On the other hand, because the abilities of nitrification and denitrification of granular sludge are limited by the size of granules (Li et al., 2012), it has been generally suggested that when the diameter is greater than 0.8 mm, dispersion of the internal dissolved oxygen (DO) will be limited, anaerobic zone can be formed inside the granules. There are more large-size granules in R1 reactor, among which the granules with the diameter of greater than 0.8 mm accounted for 37.35%, which can provide larger anaerobic zone and benefit denitrification. The size of granules in

R2 is relatively small, among which the granules with the diameter of larger than 0.8 mm only accounted for 15.91%, so a strict anaerobic zone can not be formed inside granules, the activity of denitrifying microorganism can be inhibited.

With the improvement of influent NH_4^+-N concentration each time, the NH_4^+-N removal efficiency of granular sludge could be fluctuated, which could be gradually recovered over a period of time, indicating that gradually increasing of NH_4^+-N concentration could contribute to the improvement of the ability to remove NH_4^+-N and resist the external environmental changes.

In order to study the transformation process of mature aerobic denitrifying granular sludge, the 88th running cycle after reaching steady state of substrate removal by granules was investigated in order to study the changes of each nitrogen containing compound, effluent samples were taken out every 60 min to determine the content of NH_4^+-N, NO_2^--N, NO_3^--N (Figure 3).

Figure 3 revealed that the substrate degradation trends by aerobic denitrifying granular sludge were similar in R1 and R2. NH_4^+-N was degraded rapidly in the first 120 minutes, but with the occurrence of NH_4^+-N degradation, the NO_2^-N and NO_3^--N were accumulated. After 120 minutes, NH_4^+-N was removed slowly, NO_2^--N accumulation was also decreased, which had been transformed to NO_3^--N, accumulation of which was increased gradually. The content of NH_4^+-N maintained stable in 240 – 360 min, Influent NO_2^--N content was less than 2 mg/L, accumulation rate was lower than 4%, while the accumulation of NO_3^--N still maintained in a certain amount, demonstrating that the nitrogen was removed in the reactors through the traditional process of nitrification and denitrification. The accumulation rate of NO_2^--N was quite small, which showed that NOB in aerobic nitrifying granules had higher activity.

In the first 120 min of the running cycle, DO was sufficient in the reactors because of the higher organic concentration, which make the nitrifying bacteria become very active, therefore, a majority of NH_4^+-N and COD were degraded, indicating that nitrifying bacteria and heterotro-phic bacteria were in the same dominant position for competing dissolved oxygen. While the demand of heterotrophic microorganisms for DO was also reduced accordingly after a great amount of COD were degraded, and the rest of the organic matter was insufficient to support the denitrification reaction, subsequently, denitrification process was difficult to carry on in the absence of additional carbon source, which contribute to the increasing of

NO_3^--N accumulation (Wang et al., 2008).

3. Microbial community structures of nitrifying granules

The sludge samples of two kinds of seed sludge and the mature aerobic denitrifying granules were analyzed using 16S rDNA molecular biological technique, the DGGE profiles were shown in Figure 4. The labels of inoculated R1 and inoculated R2 represented the inoculation sludge samples, the labels of R1 and R2 represented the mature aerobic denitrifying granules.

The microbial community changed dramatically among the aerobic nitrifying granules cultivated with different inoculated sludge (Figure 4). The species and quantity of dominant microorganisms in R1 were more abundant than that in R2, the increasing numbers of band in R1 demonstrated that there had been some new clonies generated or more quantities increased, such as band 2, 3, 4, 6, 8, 14, 15 and so on, while some groups had been decreased or disappeared, such as band 16, and there were also some groups with insignificant changes, such as band 7 and 13, there were 10 groups of dominant microorganisms included in the aerobic nitrifying granules that were represented as band 1, 2, 3, 4, 6, 8, 13, 14, 15.

The variances of band in R2 were not obvious, indicating that the changes of microbial community structure in R2 were smaller, the quantities of microorganisms represented as band 9 and 13 were increased, the microbial groups represented as band 7, 8 and 10 were always existing and the changes of quantities were smaller, the microbial group represented as band 6 was disappeared in the culturing process, there were 6 groups of dominant microorganisms included in the aerobic nitrifying granules that were represented as band 7, 8, 9, 10, 12, 13.

The 16 major bands in Figure 3 were sequenced after gel extraction, amplification, and cloning, the strains with the highest sequence similarity were listed in Table 3 after sequence alignment.

According to the results of sequence alignment, the main microbial groups in R1 were *Propionicimonas paludicola*, *Beggiatoa* sp., *Hyphomicrobium* sp., *Pseudomonas* sp., *Enterobacter* sp., *Sphingobium vulgare*, *Bacteroides* sp., *Clostridium bifermentans*, and these microbes were directly related to the physico-chemical properties and degradation capacities of the aerobic denitrifying granular sludge in R1.

Propionicimonas paludicola belong to a kind of common anaerobic bacteria in granules, which play a significant role in degradation of organic matter.

Propionicimonas paludicola enriched in the granules had directly contributed to the increased COD removal rate that from 78.47% in inoculation to 95.76% in mature phase. *Beggiatoa* sp. is a kind of filamentous bacteria regarded as the skeleton of the granules in the sewage treatment system, which play an important role in the construction and stability of granules, zoogloea adhere to the surface of the bacteria, due to which the granules will be formed under a variety of selection pressures. *Hyphomicrobium* sp. has been verified to possess the ability to remove nitrogen (Fesefeldt et al., 1998) in the study of related denitrifying genes. *Pseudomonas* sp. is a kind of widespread denitrifying bacteria genera in nature, there were a dozen or dozens of species in *Pseudomonas* sp. possess the ability of denitrification, which have played a key role in nitrogen removal in R1, the efficiency of nitrogen removal in R1 was significantly better than that in R2 because of the enrichment of *Pseudomonas* sp. in R1. It has been reported that the toxic tolerant capacity of *Enterobacter* sp. can be increased by means of increasing the size of the individual cells of *Enterobacter* sp. (Neumann et al., 2005), *Enterobacter* sp. enriched in the granules plays an active role in resistance to toxic and inhibitor containing wastewater. *Sphingobium vulgare* bacteria can produce polymer (Venugopalan et al., 2004) that play an important role in promoting the aggregation, formation of the granules and keeping the stability of the granular sludge, which was consistent with the changes of EPS content of granules, indicating that the increasing of bacteria groups can contribute to the significant increasing of EPS content. *Bacteroides* sp. is a kind of phosphorous removal bacteria that can remove nitrogen and phosphorous simultaneously through the processes of denitrification and anaerobic phosphorous release. *Clostridium bifermentans* is a kind of gram-positive bacteria with the ability of degrading tetrachloroethylene and halogenated aliphatic compounds (Chang et al., 2000).

The changes of bands in R2 were smaller than that in inoculated R2, indicating that the microbial community structure had little change. The microorganisms in mature aerobic nitrifying granules in R2 were represented as band 7, 8, 9, 10, 12 and 13, which include *Bacterium* PFCr-1 that can degrade organic matters, *Enterobacter* sp. that can resist to the toxic and inhibitor containing wastewater, *Chitinophaga* sp. that can transform nitrite nitrogen, *Stenotrophomonas* sp. with the ability of denitrification and *Sphingobium vulgare* bacteria with the ability of aggregation. The existence of these bacteria groups contributed to keeping a good bio-degradation effect in R2, however, its nitrogen removal effect was a bit poor compared with R1.

The species and quantities of dominant microorganisms in R1 were more abundant than that in R2, due to which the physicochemical properties and degradability of granules in R1 were superior to that of granules in R2. Therefore, the sludge from beer wastewater treatment plant was proved to be more suitable for inoculation to culture the aerobic nitrifying granules.

E.g.5: Results

1. MNPs-producing strain isolation and identification

Transmission electron microscope (TEM) observation (Figure 1) shows that the cells are short rod in morphology with a mean width of 0.5 μm and a mean length of 1.2 μm. They were uniflagellate bacteria with several flagellum at one pole. And one or two nanoparticles were identified in each cell. The cell yield of YN01 is about 1.14×10^{11} cells/L (growth medium). Chromosomal DNA was prepared from the bacterial culture, and 16S rDNA genes were amplied for identification as described previously (Schüler et al., 1999). According to a sequence homology analysis of Genbank by BLAST program, this novel MNPs-producing bacteria strain was identified as *Burkholderia* sp., named as YN01.

2. Preparation and characterization of the BMNPs extracted from YN01

The magnetic nanoparticles in bacterial cells were separated and purified following procedures of ultrasonication, ultracentrifugation and magnet adsorption. The BMNPs productivity is about 1.89 mg/L (growth medium). The BMNPs were identified as pure face-centered cubic phase of magnetite (Fe_3O_4) (JCPDS 019-0629) by X-ray diffraction (XRD) showed in Figure 2A. TEM image (Figure 3) reveals that the size distribution of the crystals is uniform and the average size is about 80 nm. X-ray photoelectron spectroscopy (XPS) was employed to further explore the composition of the BMNPs purified from YN01. As shown in Figure 4A, there are three major elements that are Fe 2p, O 1s and C 1s in the surface of BMNPs according to the wide spectrum. The photoelectron peaks at 711.2 eV and 724.5 eV are the characteristic doublets of Fe $2p^{3/2}$ and Fe $2p^{1/2}$ according to the narrow spectrum of Fe 2p (Figure 4B). The charactersitic peaks at 532.2 eV and 284.6 eV of O 1s and C 1s are showed in Figure 4C,D. The hysteresis loop of the BMNPs samples is potbellied as shown in Figure 5 and the values of hysteresis parameters such as B_c and B_{cr} and ratios $M_{rs}/$

M_s were deduced as 35.6 mT, 43.2 mT and 0.47 respectively.

3. Peroxidase-like activity of the BMNPs

As illustrated in Figure 6, we found that BMNPs could catalyze the oxidation of peroxidase substrate 3,3',5,5' – tetramethylbenzidine (TMB) in the presence of H_2O_2 to produce a blue color reaction with maximum absorbance of the reaction mixture at 652 nm (Josephy et al., 1982). In contrast, both the solution of TMB and H_2O_2 in the absence of BMNPs and the solution of TMB and BMNPs in the absence of H_2O_2 showed no oxidation reaction, showing that both the components are required for the oxidative reaction, as observed for horseradish peroxidase (HRP) (Josephy et al., 1982; Chattopadhyay et al., 2000). Additionally, the TMB oxidation rate catalyzed by BMNPs is dependent on their concentration, the reaction rate increased with increasing BMNPs concentration as shown in Figure 7A. The composition and phase of BMNPs remained unchanged after the peroxidase reaction according to XRD patterns (Figure 2B). The BMNPs were incubated in the reaction buffer for 10 min and then removed from the solution using a magnet to prepare a leaching solution. Online Resource 1 showed that the leaching solution had no activity.

4. Effect of pH, temperature and H_2O_2 concentration on BMNPs activity

The peroxidase-like activity of BMNPs was measured while varying the pH from 1 to 8, the temperature from 25 ℃ to 60 ℃, H_2O_2 concentration from 0.001 to 2 M. The maximum catalytic activity of BMNPs was obtained under the following optimal conditions: pH 3.8, 30 ℃, 200 mM H_2O_2, the reaction time was set as 5 min. (Figure 7).

5. Kinetic analysis of BMNPs activity

The peroxidase-like catalytic activity of BMNPs was investigated using steady-state kinetics and the typical Michaelis-Menten curves were shown in Figure 8A, B. The kinetic data were obtained by varying one substrate concentration while keeping the other substrate concentration constant. A series of initial reaction rates were calculated and applied to the double reciprocal of the Michaelis-Menten equation, $1/v = (K_m/V_{max}) \cdot (1/[S]) + 1/V_{max}$, where v is the initial velocity, $[S]$ is the concentration of the substrate, K_m is the Michaelies – Menten constant and V_{max} is the maximal reaction velocity. The K_m, V_{max} and K_{cat} values (Online Resource 6) were obtained using Lineweaver-Burk plots. To further investigate the mechanism of BMNPs catalysis, their activity over a range of TMB and H_2O_2 concentrations was measured. The double reciprocal plots of initial velocity against the concentration of one substrate were obtained over a range of concentrations of the other (Figure 8C, D).

6. Study of free radical formation by ESR

ESR technique was employed to investigate the possible mechanism by determining free radical formation induced by BMNPs in the presence of H_2O_2. In the results of this study, the ESR spectra in the presence of BMNPs displayed a 4-fold characteristic peak of the typical DMPO/·OH adduct with an intensity ratio of 1:2:2:1. There is no DMPO/·OH adduct signal intensity in the control experement in the absence of BMNPs (Figure 9).

7. Electrochemical analysis of the origin of BMNPs activity

The electrocatalytic behavior of BMNPs nanoparticles modified glassy carbon electrode (GCE) towards reduction of H_2O_2 was examined using cyclic voltammetry in standard conditions, demonstrating clearly that no obvious current was found in the absence of H_2O_2, but an obvious current was observed in the presence of H_2O_2 (Figure 10A). The amperometric response of the BMNPs modified GCE to H_2O_2 was shown in Figure 10B. The reduction current increased steeply to reach a steady state value with upon addition of an aliquot of H_2O_2 to the buffer solution.

8. Comparison of stability of peroxidase activity of BMNPs and HRP

To examine and compare the robustness of peroxidase activity of BMNPs and HRP, both BMNPs and HRP were exposed to a range of values of pH and a range of temperatures for 2 h, and then measured their activities under standard conditions (pH 3.8 and 30 ℃). The catalytic activity of HRP was largely inhibited after treatment at pH lower than 4 or temperature higher than 50 ℃ (Online Resource 2A, B). In contrast, the catalytic activity of BMNPs remained stable over a wide range of pH from 2 to 12 and temperature from 4 ℃ to 70 ℃ (Online Resource 2A, B).

9. H_2O_2 and glucose detection

The absorbance at 652 nm is proportional to H_2O_2 concentrations from 0.01 to

8 mM with a detection limit (DL) of 0.005 mM (Online Resource 3A). Because H_2O_2 is the main product of glucose oxidase (GO_x)-catalyzed reaction, when the catalytic reaction by BMNPs is combined with the glucose catalytic reaction by GO_x, the proposed colorimetric method could be used to determine glucose. The linear range for glucose is from 0.01 to 5 mM and the DL is 0.005 mM (Online Resource 3B), which can be potentially applied to detect glucose in diluted serum. The specificity to glucose of the proposed colorimetric method was investigated using fructose, lactose and maltose. The results demonstrated that these glucose analogues were even at concentration as high as 5 mM, no detectable signals of the control samples was observed compared with that of glucose (Online Resource 4).

10. Phenol and congo red dye degradation

As shown in Online Resource 5A, the BMNPs were able to efficiently degrade phenol at pH 3.8 and temperature 30 ℃, about 68% of phenol was degraded after 25 min by 100 mg/L BMNPs, and the phenol degradation rate increased with time increasing, and the time to achieve the same degradation rate was significantly reduced with the increasing of BMNPs concentration. Online Resource 5B demonstrated that nearly 60% degradation for Congo red dye by 200 mg/mL BMNPs was observed during 10 min, and the degradation rate was also BMNPs concentration dependent. The effect of BMNPs recycling times on degradation rate was demonstrated in Online Resource 5C, the degradation rate gradually decreased with the BMNPs recycling time increasing. When the BMNPs had been reused for seven times, the degradation rate of both phenol and Congo red decreased by about 15% compared with that in the first time, which might be due to the loss of BMNPs in the recycling and washing processes.

E. g. 6: Discussion

It is well known that magnetic nanoparticles (MNPs) are of particular interest because of their dual functionality as a peroxidase mimetic and a magnetic separation agent (Gao et al., 2007; Morishita et al., 2005). Recently, biosynthesis of MNPs has become a useful technique in the place of traditional chemical procedures which are known to employ high temperatures and pressure, hazardous organic solvents. In contrast, the development of eco-friendly and green-synthesis approaches to synthesize MNPs using microorganisms have gained considerable attention although microbial synthesis still has some challenges to overcome and some issues to explore, such as the better control of nanoparticle sizes and shapes (Durán et al., 2012; Seabra et al., 2013). Some microorganisms are believed to produce ferromagnetic nanoparticles with single-domain and uniform particle size, for instance, magnetotactic bacteria (Bazylinski et al., 2004; Matsunaga et al., 2007; Dutz et al., 2009) and non-magnetotactic bacteria (Vainshtein et al., 2002). Compared with AMNPs, the biogenic MNPs would be expected to show superior performances (Knopp et al., 2009). Here, we have isolated a novel MNPs-producing bacteria strain identified as *Burkholderia* sp. YN01, extracted MNPs from YN01 were characterized as face-centered cubic 80 nm Fe_3O_4 with ferromagnetic behavior. According to the XRD patterns of the BMNPs from YN01, the seven characteristic diffraction peaks in the range of $15 < 2\theta < 65$ can be indexed as pure face-centered cubic Fe_3O_4 (JCPDS 019-0629), and the sharp peaks indicate that the product is well crystallized (Han et al., 2007). The unchanged XRD patterns reveal that the BMNPs composition remains unchanged after catalytic reaction, which is in accordance with natural enzymes. In order to further confirm the fact that the BMNPs extracted from YN01 were identified as Fe_3O_4 MNPs, XPS data were collected in this study. The survey showed the presence of Fe 2p, C 1s, O 1s originating from BMNPs, indicating that there are three elements that are Fe, O and C. The element C in the surface of BMNPs may be mainly from the label carbon in the process of instrument detection. In the XPS survey, the narrow spectrums of the three elements were also provided, the photoelectron peaks at 711.2 and 724.5 eV should originate from 2p orbital electron transition of Fe atom in BMNPs and there is a smooth curve rather than satellite peaks between the two peak positions, which is consistent with the XPS spectrum of Fe_3O_4 NPs reported previously (Yamashita and Hayes 2008). This is the first report concerning on biogenic Fe_3O_4 NPs produced in *Burkholderia* genus.

Artificial magnetic nanoparticles (AMNPs) have been demonstrated to have peroxidase-like activity comparable with those exhibited by horseradish peroxidase (HRP) (Gao et al., 2007) and MNPs-magnetosomes synthesis in bacterial protecting the cell from H_2O_2 toxicity was pointed by Blakemore (1982), the bacterial magnetosomes in *M. gryphiswaldense* MSR-1 exhibiting peroxidase-like activity to reduce intracellular reactive oxygen species (ROS) levels was also observed by Guo et al. (2012). It is well known that peroxidase can catalyze the oxidation of peroxidase substrates to produce a color change (Josephy et al., 1982; Chattopadhyay et al.,

2000). In order to investigate the peroxidase-like activity of the extracted BMNPs from YN01, similar experiments were carried out. We confirm for the first time that this BMNPs purified from *Burkholderia* sp. YN01 can be evaluated as peroxidase mimetics. As expected, the catalytic activity of the BMNPs is depen-dent on pH, temperature and H_2O_2 concentration, similar to HRP (Josephy et al., 1982; Chattopadhyay et al., 2000). The optimal temperature and pH are similar to that observed with other NPs-based mimetics and HRP (Gao et al., 2007; Dai et al., 2009; André et al., 2010; Mu et al., 2012; Chaudhari et al., 2012; Song et al., 2010; Shi et al., 2011). However, the enzymatic activity of BMNPs at pH 7.4 is only 6.8% of the maximum activity at pH 3.8, which can be a serious limitation for their biological applications, such as H_2O_2, glucose, GSH detection in real biological samples (blood, adenocarcinoma epithelial cell lines and so on). Our results suggested that the BMNPs required a H_2O_2 concentration about two orders of magnitude higher than HRP to reach the maximum level of peroxidase activity, which indicates that the catalytic activity of BMNPs is more stable at high H_2O_2 concentration than that of HRP (Chattopadhyay et al., 2000). However, inhibition of the peroxidase-like activity of BMNPs was found when further increasing the H_2O_2 concentration, as is observed for the enzyme catalyzed reaction. The apparent K_m value of BMNPs with H_2O_2 as the substrate is significantly higher than that of HRP, in agreement with the observation that a higher H_2O_2 concentration is required to achieve maximal activity for BMNPs. And the apparent K_m value of BMNPs with TMB as the substrate is much smaller than HRP, suggesting that the BMNPs have a higher affinity for TMB than that of HRP, which may be due to the presence of more "active nanostructures". Observed parallel lines in the results of steady-state kinetic assay are the characteristic of a ping-pong mechanism, indicating that the BMNPs nanoparticles bind and react with the first substrate, then release the first product before reacting with the second one, as observed for HRP (Josephy et al., 1982). In our study, BMNPs were also proved to be more stable than natural peroxidase like HRP. The stability of BMNPs in wide pH and temperature ranges makes them suitable under harsh conditions and is crucial to extend their potential applications.

Iron and other free metal ions are important cofactors for antioxidant defence enzymes, e.g. catalase, peroxidase and SOD (Agranoff and Krishna, 1998; Nelson, 1999; Horsburgh et al., 2001). In order to test that the observed peroxidase – like activity of BMNPs is due to the intact nanoparticles and not the free metal ions leaching into solution, the BMNPs were incubated in the reaction buffer for 10 min and then removed from the solution using a magnet to prepare a leaching solution. Our experimental results demonstrated that the observed peroxidase-like activity results from the surface properties of the nanostructure and not from the ion-leaching process.

The molecular level mechanisms responsible for iron oxide as peroxidase mimics have not been completely determined (Wei et al., 2013). As reported previously, the peroxidase-like activity of iron oxides nanoparticles may originate following Fenton's reaction mechanism because of the presence of ferrous ions at the surface of the nanoparticles (Chen et al., 2012; Chaudhari et al., 2012). In this study, the nature of peroxidase-like activity of BMNPs that may originate from their catalytic ability to H_2O_2 decomposition into ·OH radicals was confirmed with the ESR technique. The results provide direct evidence that H_2O_2 alone did not produce hydroxyl radicals, however, addition of BMNPs assisted the formation of hydroxyl radicals from H_2O_2. It has been suggested that iron oxides NPs transfer electron between pairs of different oxidation states of Fe^{2+}/Fe^{3+} to drive their catalytic activity (Shi et al., 2011). In the present system, H_2O_2 molecules can be adsorbed on the surface of BMNPs and then activated by the bound Fe^{2+} and Fe^{3+} to generate the ·OH radical. The generated ·OH radical might be stabilized by BMNPs through partial electron exchange interaction, which may contribute to the catalytic ability of BMNPs.

The electrochemical sensor for H_2O_2 using Fe_3O_4 NPs as peroxidase mimic was reported (Zhang et al., 2011). The results suggested that the Fe_3O_4 NPs modified electrode had better response than the bare electrode by accelerating electron transfer. We also studied the electrocatalytic behavior of BMNPs towards H_2O_2 reduction. The results are consistent with the above, therefore, we can conclude that the BMNPs have the ability of electron transfer between electrode (electron donor) and H_2O_2 (electron acceptor) in the electrochemical process above, exhibiting an electrocatalytic activity to H_2O_2 reduction, which may be also associated with the nature of the catalytic activity of BMNPs.

Because the catalytic activity of the BMNPs is H_2O_2 concentration dependent in a certain range, this can be used for H_2O_2 detection, and the demonstrated biosensing system in our study is highly selective for glucose owing to the high affinity of glucose oxidase for glucose. The natural peroxidase, such as HRP, which possesses the ability to catalyze the oxidation of aromatic compound in the presence of H_2O_2 has been widely applied in the treatment of phenolic wastewater (Wright and Necell, 1999; Enda et al., 1996), and it is also reported that azo-dyes family can also be used as peroxidase substrates (Zhu et al., 1997). According to our study, BMNPs were also proved to have the ability to degrade phenol and Congo red dye as a novel peroxidase mimetic.

13.5.2　Useful expressions and sectence patterns

As (is) shown in Figure X	如图 X 所示
As (is) presented in Figure X	如图 X 所示
As (is) listed in Table X	列于表 X
As (is) given in Table X	列于表 X
It can be seen from Figure X that...	由图 X 可见……
It is evident from Figure X that...	由图 X 可明显看出……
As is clear from Figure X that...	由图 X 可明显看出……
From Figure X it is apparent that...	由图 X 可明显看出……
increase with...	随……增加
decrease with...	随……降低
change with...	随……变化
vary with...	随……变化
The effect of... on... is shown in Figure 3	……对……的影响示于图 3
The higher..., the higher...	……越高,……也越高
In order to investigate the effect of... on...	为了研究……对……的影响
Contrast to...	和……相比

表明结果的短语有：

The results indicated that...

As a result...

It turns out that...

It has been found that...

The results show that...

We conclude that...

It may be noted that...

13.6 Conclusion

结论是在文章的结尾对研究结果条理化,是论文的总观点,告诉读者这篇论文解决了什么问题。结论不应是正文中各段小结的简单重复,它应该以正文中的实验或考察中得到的现象、数据和阐述分析作为依据,由此完整、准确、简洁地指出:

(1)由对研究对象进行考察或实验得到的结果所揭示的原理及其普遍性;
(2)研究中有无发现例外或本论文尚难以解释和解决的问题;
(3)与先前已经发表过的(包括他人或著者自己)研究工作的异同;
(4)本论文在理论上与实用上的意义与价值;
(5)对进一步深入研究本课题的建议。

有的论文将 Conclusion 隐含在"Results and Discussion"中,不单独设一小节。

下面是几篇科技论义的结论部分:

E.g.1:In summary, different types of low molecular weight organic acids had different ability to release P from both rock phosphate and iron phosphate. P release from rock phosphate is mainly related to the acid strength (pH) of the organic acid as well as the complex and chelating effects; while P release from iron phosphate is largely due to the complex and chelating effects of the organic acid. Increase in solution pH had much more pronounced effect on P solubilization from rock phosphate than from phosphate. Addition of phenolic compounds increase P solubilization from iron phosphate.

E.g.2:In summary, we have demonstrated for the first time that magnetic nanoparticles can be produced in *Burkholderia* genus and the extracted BMNPs from *Burkholderia* sp. YN01 were characterized and proved to be novel peroxidase mimetics. Furthermore, we also show that the BMNPs could be used for colorimetric determination of H_2O_2 and glucose and high efficiency in phenol and Congo red dye degradation by BMNPs was obtained under optimal catalytic conditions. This work will provide new information of biogenic magnetic nanoparticles as peroxidase mimetics and facilitate their utilization in bioassays and catalytic elimination of environmental pollutants.

E.g.3:The bioreactor was suitable to the development of nitrifying activity and the accumulation of nitrifying activated sludge. After ran aerobically for 51 d, volumetric ammonia loading rate reached 56.96 mmol/(L·d) and volumetric conversion rate reached 56.85 mmol/(L · d). Nitrifying activated sludge could serve as seeding sludge to start up Anammox bioreactor. Anammox bioreactor was highly efficient with total nitrogen volumetric removal rate of 149.55 mmol/(L · d), and its performance was very stable that a large fluctuation(23.6%) of volumetric total nitrogen loading rate only led to a small change(7.3%) of total nitrogen removal. Soft padding helped to remain Anammox sludge in the bioreactor effectively. The biomass loss from washout was small with average effluent VSS concentration as low as 0.023 g/L.

E.g.4: Biodegradation in biofilter containing compost as the main biomass support appears to be a cost effective treatment method for easily biodegradable volatile compounds like ethanol and methanol. The continuous studies on biodegradation of mixture of ethanol and methanol vapours in biofilter with acclimatized biomass have revealed the feasibility of treating these compounds under extended period of operation with preferential removal of ethanol over methanol. Both the removals of ethanol and methanol were comparatively less than those for the pure compounds. The effect on ethanol removal was due to the inhibitory effect of methanol on ethanol utilizing organisms while the effect on methanol removal was due to preferential utilization of ethanol by methanol utilizing microorganisms. Appreciable elimination rates of both ethanol and methanol were obtained at lower proportion of methanol to ethanol. This study established the potential application of biofilters for the treatment of VOCs.

E.g.5: ACF can be used with packed bed for removal of gas phase TCE at low concentration. The breakthrough characteristics depended on both the ACF's properties and the operation conditions. It was found that the breakthrough time increased with the increasing specific surface area, decreased with increasing operating temperature or humidity. It was important that the breakthrough curves at various inlet concentrations or temperatures can be predicted by several simple models with good agreements. It suggested that we could obtain the breakthrough behaviors under certain condition.

E.g.6: The application of MCIs in the prediction of physic-chemical properties of persistent organic pollutants was extended in this study. A series of QSPR equations were established with high significance and accuracy, which shows this simple approach is effective and applicable in the estimation for properties needed for the risk assessment and exposure evaluation.

E. g. 7: Reaction between ClO_2 and aniline was the first-order with respect to both ClO_2 and aniline, and the overall reaction was of second order. The Stoichiometric factor η was 2.44. Under condition of pH 6.86 and Tw287 K, the reaction rate constant k was 0.11 L/(mol·s). Activation energy of the reaction was 72.31 kJ/mol, revealing that the reaction could take place under usual water processing conditions. Reaction rate constants in acidic and alkali media were greater than that in neutral medium. Therefore, acidic and alkali media were favorable for the reaction to neutral condition. In neutral and alkali media chlorite ion could hardly react with aniline. It could oxide aniline in acidic medium, but the effect of it on the rate constant of reaction between ClO_2 and aniline was insignificant.

E. g. 8: The activated sludge from beer and municipal wastewater treatment plants was used as seed sludge to culture the aerobic nitrifying granules in R1 and R2 respectively. The granules possess superior performances of good settleability, high bioactivity, strong hydrophobicity and stability. After cultivation in R1 and R2, the SVI values of mature granules could reach 21.39 mL/g and 23.87 mL/g respectively, the SOUR value was more than 1.1 mgO_2/gMLVSS·min, Zeta potential values were 3.926 mV and 5.049 mV respectively, EPS content was increased to more than 160 mg/gVSS, PN/PS ratio could reach 1.91 and 1.88, the removal rate of NH_4^+-N were 89.42% and 75.69% respectively.

The results of nitrogen transformation process in cycle operation demonstrated that the majority of NH_4^+-N was removed in the first 120 min, NO_2^--N had a certain amount of accumulation in the first 120 min, then the accumulation amount reduced gradually, NO_2^--N accumulation in effluent was quite small that was less than 2 mg/L, there was a certain amount of accumulation of NO_3^--N in the effluent.

According to the analysis of 16S rDNA sequence, the microbial community structure of cultured aerobic nitrifying granules differed dramatically among the different seed sludge. The aerobic nitrifying granules cultivated by the seed sludge with abundant communities possessed better performances. The aerobic nitrifying granules cultivated by activated sludge from beer wastewater treatment plant contained 10 dominant groups, which include *Bggiatoa* sp. that was regarded as skeleton of granules, *Sphingobium vulgare* that can produce eupolymer, *Propionicimonas paludicola* that can degrade organic matters, *Enterobacter* sp. that has the ability to resist to the toxic and inhibitor containing wastewater, *Pseudomonas* sp. and *Bacteroides* sp. with the ability of denitrification.

13.7 Acknowledgments

研究工作通常不是一个或几个人的力量所能完成的,它需要有关单位和个人的指导、支持和帮助,因此,作者有必要在致谢部分对给予支持和帮助的单位和个人表示感谢。文章中的致谢多置于结论之后,参考文献之前。

对于向对自己有帮助的人表示感谢,可以有很多表达方式和用语,但它最基本的内容是向谁致谢和致谢的原因,最基本的形式是以致谢者或者意愿为主语(也可省去致谢者),对被感谢者使用"to + 被感谢者"这种结构,感谢的原因用"for..."来表达。举例如下。

Acknowledgements: The authors appreciate Prof. Wang for PC strain and NJYZ for the PTA wastewater and YZ.I strain.

Acknowledgements: The authors are grateful to Dr. X. P. Huang and Dr. D. C. Wang for their help on the sampling program.

Acknowledgements: The authors would like to thank Sha Luqing, Fu Xianhui, Wang Hong and Li Qingjun, from Xishuangbanna Tropical Botanical Garden, Chinese Academy of Sciences(CAS), for their assistance in soil sampling. We wish to thank Mrs. Zhang Shumin and Yu Fenglan for their help in laboratory analysis, and we also thank Mr. Cai Ruiguo and Liu Fangchun from Shandong Agricultural University for their help in soil sample analysis.

Acknowledgement: The author is greatly acknowledged the constant encouragement and guidance from Dr. N. M. Nifndeokar, Head Chemistry Department and staff.

Acknowledgements: The authors thank Dr. B. Wood of the Department of Chemistry for the XPS measurements, and Mr. L. K. Bekessy of the Department of Mining and Material Engineering for XRD measurements.

Acknowledgements: The authors wish to express their appreciation to the Analytical Center at Jiangsu Institute of Technology for the measurement of pore size distribution. Thanks the Analytical Center at Yancheng Teachers College for the HPLC analysis.

某些论文是在某个机构经费的资助下完成的,在发表论文时,需要向资助单位致谢。具体的例子如下:

Acknowledgements: The authors gratefully acknowledge the financial support of this work by the Project KJCXGC – 01 of Northwest Normal University, Lanzhou and the Project of Youth Teachers Foundation of education of Ministry, China.

Acknowledgements: Author thanks Dr. R. Y. H. Cheung and Professor M. H. Wong for their guidance and advice. Financial support from the City University of Hong Kong is gratefully acknowledged.

Acknowledgements: The authors would like to take the opportunity to thank Deakin University, Australia and the program of Yunnan Provincial Office of Science and Technology, China for their support of the project.

Acknowledgements: The authors would like to thank Bangladesh University Grants Commission for financial support for carrying out this research.

Acknowledgements: The authors wish to thank The Hong Kong University Development Fund for the partial financial support of this project. Ke Shui zhou wishes to thank The Hong Kong University for providing him the Visitorship.

13.8 References

在科技论文的后面列举参考文献是科技论文写作的一项很重要的内容,它不仅是为方便读者查阅,其重要性还在于明确地标示出引用他人的学术思想、理论、成果和数据的部分,并给出其来源,以体现文献的继承性和对他人成果的尊重,又表明了学术的严肃性。凡是在论文中引用别人的文章、观点或研究结果,都应该标注,以表明其出处。论文所列的参考文献应该只限于那些作者亲自阅读过和论文中引用过,而且都是读者能够查阅到的公开出版物上的文献或其他有关档案资料。内部讲义及未发表的著作,一般不宜作为参考文献著录。参考文献可以是期刊论文、专著、教材、研究报告、学位论文、会议论文、专利等。

参考文献和论文的引言是紧密相连的,现代科学技术研究工作都是在前人已完成的工作基础上进行的,科技工作者在进行一项科研工作时,最基础的工作就是文献的检索工作,通过检索工作,查询他人在此方面都做了哪些研究工作,进而了解他人工作的进展和进度,以及他人的研究工作是否具有以及具有哪些局限性。所以在写作论文时,在前言中应概述他人的工作,并指出他人工作与本论文工作有哪些联系和不同,以及本论文希望在哪些方面取得进展,其中提到他人的工作时,一定要给出参考文献,做到言之有据,所以文后的参考文献可以从一个方面反映出作者参考资料的情况,进而反映出该论文的学术水平。如果论文后的参考文献都是国内已出版很久的图书,说明作者参考的都是一些很旧的文献,作者的知识陈旧,所写出的论文就很难有较高的学术水平;如果论文后的参考文献都是作者通过国际著名检索机构查询到的国际上该领域的最新成果,则说明作者参考了大量的最新文献,作者的研究工作处于该领域的前沿,论文被国际著名检索机构收录的机会就会大大增加,所以建议在查询文献时,要充分利用国际著名检索机构,查询国内外一些著名核心期刊所发表的论文以做参考。

在文后标注参考文献时,必须符合一定的要求。不同的科技期刊所要求的参考文献的格式并不完全相同,因此,投稿前应先了解所投期刊对参考文献编排格式的要求,按照它的具体要求编排。

目前国内外科技期刊在标注参考文献时,一般采用顺序编码标注制。采用顺序编码标注制时,参考文献应按论文中引用的先后顺序从1开始连续编号。正文中的编号一般用方括号括起来,放在引用文献的作者或引用的内容之后。如果同一个地方引用多篇文献,需将各篇文献的序号在方括号内全部列出,各序号间用逗号隔开;如果遇到连续序号,可用符号"～"连接,略去中间序号;如果需要为整段内容注明参考文献,编号应放在此段最后一句的后面。参考文献中文献的排列顺序应与论文中引用的顺序相同。

采用顺序编码标注制时,参考文献的著录项目与著录格式参考如下。

连续出版物:序号作者. 题名. 刊名, 出版年份, 卷号(期号):引文所在的起始或起止页码.

专著:序号作者. 书名. 版本(第1版不标注), 出版地:出版者, 出版年.

论文集:序号作者. 题名. 见(英文用 In):主编. 论文集名. 出版地:出版者, 出版年. 引文所在起始或起止页码.

学位论文:序号作者. 题名:[博士或硕士学位论文]. 保存地点:保存单位, 年份.

专利:序号专利申请者. 题名. 专利国别, 专利文献种类, 专利号. 出版日期.

技术标准:序号起草责任者. 标准代号标准顺序号—发布年标准名称. 出版地:出版者, 出版年.

电子文献:序号作者. 电子文献题名. 电子文献的网址.

会议文献、科技报告的著录项目与著录格式均可按专著著录。

如下面这些例子:

E. g. 1: Hoffman M, Martin S, Choi W, et al. Environmental application of semiconductor photocatalysis [J]. Chem. Rev., 1995, 95: 69.

E. g. 2: Alberici R M, Jardim W F. Photocatalytic degradation of phenol and chlorinated phenols using Ag – TiO_2 in a slurry reactor [J]. Water Res., 1994, 28: 1845.

E. g. 3: An T C, Zhu X H, Xiong Y. Synergic degradation of reactive brilliant red X – 3B using three dimension electrode-photocatalytic reactor [J]. J. Envion. Sci. Health, 2001, 36A (10): 2069.

E. g. 4: Navio J A, Testa J J, Djedjeian P, et al. Iron-doped titania powders by a sol-gel methods. Part Ⅱ: photocatalytic properties [J]. Appl. Catal. A: General, 1999, 178: 191.

E. g. 5: An T C, Zhu X H, Xiong Y. Feasibility study of photoelectrochemical degradation of methylene blue with three dimensional electro-des-photocatalytic reactor [J]. Chemosphere, 2002, 46 (6): 897.

E. g. 6: Doug L. Study on decolor of dyeing wastewater by chlorine dioxide [D]. Paper for Master's Degree of Harbin Institute of Architecture Engineering,1999.

E. g. 7: Karel V. Handbook of Environmental data on organic chemicals (2nd Ed.) [M]. New York, Van Nostrand Reinhold Company Inc. , 1983, 356, 1110.

E. g. 8: Verwey E J W, Overbeek J T G. Theory of the stability of lyophobic colloids[M] . New York :Elsevier. Publishing Co. , 1948.

E. g. 9: Schecher W D. MINEQL A chemical equilibrium model for personal computers, users manual version 2122 [Z]. Hallowell, ME: Environ. Res Software Inc. , 1991.

E. g. 10: De S G G. Overall reaction rates of NO and N_2 formation from fuel nitrogen [A]. In : 15th Symposium International on Combustion[C]. The Combustion Institute, Pittsburgh, 1975. 1093-1102.

参考文献的写法还有一种,那就是按作者的姓名字母顺序来排列,实际上是按作者的姓的字母顺序排列,对参考文献不加序号,在引用时需写明作者姓名和出版年代。

如下面这些参考文献:

E. g. 1: Bock E, Schmidt L, Stuven R et al. ,1995. Nitrogen loss caused by denitrifyirmg Nitrosomonas cells using, ammonium or hydrogen as electron donors and nitrite as electron acceptor [J]. Arch Microbiol, 163: 16-20.

E. g. 2: Chen J S, Shi J L, Xu Y T, 1996. Measurement of nitrifying rate and nitrobacter count for application to investigating the affects of denitrification [J]. Shanghai Environmental Sciences, 15(3):18-20.

E. g. 3: China Bureau of Environmental Protection, 1997. Methods for write, and analysis of water and wastewater (3rd edition) [M]. Beijing: China Environmental Science Press.

E. g. 4: Fang S, Li X H, 2001. Performance of the short nitrifying/denitrifying process treating sodium glutamate production wastewater with high concentration of ammomium [J]. Acta. Scientiae circumstantiae, 21(1): 79-83.

E. g. 5: Hu B L, Zheng P, Guan L L, 2001. Isolation, identification and characteristics of Ammonia-oxidation bacteria from Anammox reactor [J] Journal of Zhejiang University, 27(3): 314-316.

E. g. 6: Jetten M S M, Horn S J, Van Loosdrecht MCM, 1997. Towards a more sustainable municiple wastewater treatment system [J]. Wat Sci. Tech., 35(9): 171-180.

E. g. 7: Jin Z G, Qu J N, He Q B, 1998. Study on analytical and methods of nitrifying bacteria enrichment technology [J]. Shanghai Environmental Science, 17(8): 16-18.

E. g. 8: Lovley D R, Coates J D, Saffarini D A, et al., 1997. Dissimilatory iron reduction. In: iron and related transition metals in microbial metabolism (G. Winkeloman and C. J. Carrano ed.). Switzerland: Harwood.

E. g. 9: Mao C W, 2001. A study on oxidation kinetic between chlorine dioxide and phenolic compounds and their quatitative structure activity relationship [D]. Thesis for PhD candidate of HIT.

E. g. 10: Zhang J L, 2000. Analytical Technique of chlorine dioxide [M]. Beijing: China Environmental Science Press.

Exercise

(1)请将下列句子译成汉语。

In recent years, the study of special properties of metal catalysts supported on composite oxides has aroused great attention. These works mainly concentrate on the interaction between the coated oxide and substrate.

It is well recognized that conventional drinking water treatment processes have low efficiency in removing tricholoethylene from water; new process must be used to ensure the health of the population.

There are several reports about ACF absorbing VOCs in drinking water, however, few researches have been done to identify the feasibility of ACF removing gas phase TCE at low concentration.

Studies concerning the influences of pesticides on soil enzyme activity have been reviewed frequently.

The factor of pollution studied was simple, while with the rapid development of industry and agriculture in world many contaminations coexist in soil and environmental problems can not be explained by simple contamination. So combined pollution comes to arouse attention and turn to one of the important research directions in environmental science.

While the main effects of combined pollutions, for example acid rain, heavy metal and atrazine, on the activities of soil enzymes have not been reported.

Soils were sampled from the surface layer (0 – 15 cm) of three agricultural fields used for rice cultivation near Jinhua City, Zhejiang province, China, after removal of surface water.

HPLC separation was performed on a C_{18} reserved-phase column, using a mixed solution as mobile phase (mixed with (v/v) 60% CH_3CN, 35% H_2O and 5% of 0.085% H_3PO_4 solution). The flow rate was 1 ml/min and injection volume was 10 μL.

The air-dry soils were sieved (1 mm) and mixed with all contaminations shown in Table 2 in flasks with enough shaking. The H^+ was mixed by sulfuric acid and nitric acid (5:1) and AL^{3+}, Cu^{2+} were added as aluminum sulfate and cupric sulfate.

Aniline, AR; ClO_2: prepared by reaction between sodium chlorite and vitriol followed by saturated sodium chlorite washing. Purity of chlorine dioxide was above 99%; pH buffer solution was prepared by mixing NaH_2PO_4 and Na_2HPO_4 solution pro rata. All other reagents were of AR.

Experiment procedure was as follows: add a certain volume of $ArNH_2$ solution with an injector into the reactor. Then start the beater and inject a certain volume of ClO_2 solution. At this time the volume of the system was about 30 mL.

Then transfer all the solution in the reactor into a 100 mL separatory funnel. Extract this solution with benzene three times (10 mL for each time). And then combine the extraction.

The photochemical reactor employed in this work is shown in Figure 1. It is a cylindrical stainless steel reactor of 80 mm inner diameter and 450 mm height, which is fixed with a low-pressure mercury vapor lamp in the axial position.

Glass beaker containing 100 cm³ aqueous dye solution placed in the thermostat to keep the temperature constant and use an external stirrer for constant stirring. All the experiment carried out at 27 ℃. The required amount of Fe(III) and H_2O_2 were added in the dye solution simultaneously. The concentration of dye was determined spectro photometrically using Shimadzu 160 A UV-Visible Spectrophotometer at 665 nm.

The breakthrough curves of 2700 mg/m³ TCE in the bed packed with different ACFs are shown in Figure 2. It is obvious that the breakthrough time increased with the increasing specific surface area, this indicates that the higher the specific area of ACF, the higher the adsorption capacity will be.

Trend analyses of activities of enzymes are listed in Table 3 and 4. The trend analysis showed that H^+ had a slight stimulative effect on catalase and the activities of urease, invertin and acid phosphatase decreased significantly with increasing concentration of H^+ or Cu^{2+}.

The results indicated that H^+, Cu^{2+} and incubation time affected the enzyme activities significantly. Moreover the H^+ affected much more than the other two.

To obtain the variation on the degradation of 4-CP by different pH, the investigation was carried out at various pH values, the results are shown in Figure 2.

It is perhaps because there are already certain carbons in particles of cast iron, which constitute micro cells with irons. When the two counterparts are matched with each other, the increase of the addition will have no effect on the rate.

The results of responses of the two species to Pb, Zn, Cu and Cd are shown in Table 4. Additions of Pb, Zn, Cu and Cd at the levels more than respective 5, 3, 5 and 1.5 μg/mL accordingly depressed the radicle elongation of both species significantly, and there were decreasing changes in the radicle lengths of both species accompanying with the increases of concentrations of the four metals.

(2) 请将下列句子翻译成英文。

但是为什么同一种污染物在不同浓度水平上会造成对海洋微藻完全不同的生物学反应,其机制如何? 低浓度的有机磷农药对微藻生长表现的刺激作用的机理,是否与高浓度的有机磷农药对微藻的毒害作用具有相似的机制,目前尚未见有关报道。

生物陶粒工艺是微污染水源水生物预处理的主要工艺形式之一。虽然国内对生物陶粒预处理技术进行了许多研究,但是多着重于在常温下的应用研究,对于低温条件下,特别是对于2 ℃以下的极低温度条件下,生物陶粒工艺对于水中污染物的去除效果如何,成为生物陶粒技术在我国北方推广应用所面临的重要问题。

目前大多数环保部门对水样的检测均采用经典的 BOD_5 测定方法. 但 BOD_5 法以及后来出现的检压式库仑法、BOD 测压法、瓦勃呼吸计法、短时日法等,均存在着耗时长、操作繁琐等缺陷。

近二三十年来,随着光纤技术的兴起与发展,光纤光化学传感器在环境监测方面的研究与应用受到国内外研究者的关注。

为了克服以上固化方法的不足,本文利用硅酸盐有机改性 PVA 的溶胶凝胶有机杂化包埋方法固化微生物菌株,以氧光化学传感器作为二次传感,制备了基于氧光导检测的 BOD 微生物传感器。

鉴于无机高分子絮凝剂存在相对分子质量较低、在水中的稳定性较差、投药量较高、产生的污泥量大、对水体中的胶体污染物质的吸附架桥能力较有机高分子絮凝剂差等缺点,无机高分子絮凝剂相互复合后仍不能克服以上缺点,所以,近年来无机－有机复合高分子的研制开发引起了人们的高度重视。

超声声化法是20世纪90年代初新发展起来的一种高效降解有机污染物的处理方法,其原理是利用超声辐照在溶液介质中产生的空化效应,使有机污染物降解并达到完全矿化。已有研究表明,超声声化法用于治理废水中难降解的有毒有机污染物,具有清洁、高效、反应条件温和、成本低等特点,是一种极具有产业前景的深度氧化技术。

受试水样为自配喹啉水溶液。将一定体积的喹啉(分析纯,北京金龙化学试剂公司生产)溶解于10 L去离子水中配成受试水样。受试水样在室温下的保存时间不超过24 h。

所用两种海洋微藻系购于中科院海洋所的三角褐指藻、青岛大扁藻。实验中采用青岛农药厂生产的质量分数为40%丙溴磷乳油,现用现配。

实验用海水取自青岛鲁迅公园附近海滨,经孔径0.45 μm的滤膜过滤后,煮沸消毒,冷却后配制培养液。用于培养微藻的三角烧瓶,预先在稀盐酸中浸泡数日,再分别用含有相应的丙溴磷浓度的培养液预平衡两次,共48 h以上,以消除实验过程中容器壁的吸附作用。

试验时,在带刻度的试管中加入适当质量浓度(本试验为40 mg/L) pH = 2(每升溶液中加入2 716 g的KH_2PO_4和2 017 mL质量分数为85%磷酸)的IDS溶液10 mL,在反应器取样口取水样约10 mL,立即盖上试管盖并摇匀,迅速记录体积并测定吸光度。测定时取5次平行样,将计算结果的平均值作为体系中臭氧的浓度。

首先需要考察气体吹脱和UV光解对喹啉去除的相对重要性,试验结果如图3所示。

从图3还可以看出,O_3/UV联合作用时喹啉的去除率要比O_3单独作用时的去除率高得多。尽管如此,不能根据上述结果将O_3直接氧化部分和·OH氧化部分分别计算出来,因为即使在O_3单独作用的情况下,水体中的氧化剂也不单纯是O_3。O_3单独作用时喹啉降解速率不高的一部分原因是由于pH值的影响(pH值由6.8下降到3.3)。

在丙溴磷的作用下,三角褐指藻和青岛大扁藻的生长受到相似的影响(结果如图1)。在低浓度的丙溴磷的作用下,微藻细胞的生长不仅没有受到抑制而且表现出生长加快的趋势,达到一定质量浓度时(青岛大扁藻0.4 mg/L;三角褐指藻0.1 mg/L),其刺激效应表现也最强烈。

将三角褐指藻和青岛大扁藻置于一系列含有丙溴磷的培养液中培养,测定其细胞生长和对应的MDA含量变化情况。结果表明(图2),在丙溴磷的作用下,两种微藻的MDA含量一直呈上升趋势,在丙溴磷引发微藻细胞生长增快时(青岛大扁藻0.2 mg/L,0.4 mg/L;三角褐指藻0.1 mg/L,0.2 mg/L,0.4 mg/L),它们的MDA水平也有不同程度的升高,当丙溴磷抑制微藻细胞生长时(青岛大扁藻0.8 mg/L,2 mg/L,6 mg/ L;三角褐指藻1 mg/L,4 mg/L,6mg/ L),其 MDA 含量则上升得更加明显,浓度增大,MDA 水平上升的幅度也增大。

我们的实验证明,在低浓度的新型有机磷农药——丙溴磷的作用下,青岛大扁藻和三角褐指藻也都出现了生长增快的现象,说明低浓度的有机磷农药对海洋微藻生长的刺激效应具有一定的普遍性。在高浓度的丙溴磷的作用下,两种微藻的生长又受到明显的抑制。

同时试验过程中考察了不同水温条件下生物陶粒反应器沿程对COD_{Mn}的去除,试验结果见图3。图3中床层深度以进水端为0计。可以看出,COD_{Mn}的去除主要集中在陶粒反应器底部进水端90 cm 的床层中,水温10 ℃时此段对COD_{Mn}的去除达到总去除量的85%,水温0.5 ℃时比例有所下降,此段COD_{Mn}的去除达到总去除量的65%。

这是由于进水端营养物相对较丰富,微生物活性强,微生物量多;而反应器顶部出水端部分,营养物相对较少,微生物生长受到限制,活性低,微生物总量稀少,因此生物陶粒反应器对污染物的去除主要集中在进水端,出水端部分基本上没有去除效果。

图2所示的实验结果是不同聚合铝(仅以$PACl_0$ 和 $PACl_{20}$为例)Al_a 形态在颗粒物与溶液中随不同 pH 条件下的变化情况。两条曲线分别为总体系所含 Al_a(包括颗粒物及溶液中的 Al_a 和颗粒物本身导致的吸光度)和滤液(即溶液)中的 Al_a 随 pH 的变化。从图中可以发现一个共同的现象:体系中的 Al_a 与滤液中 Al_a 随 pH 含量变化规律完全吻合,两线之间基本维持一不变的距离。说明滤液中的 Al_a 量近似为体系中总 Al_a 量,也就是说,颗粒物上基本不含 Al_a,两线中间的差值即为颗粒物的吸光值。这是颗粒物表面形态分布的一个主要特点。

从图1,2 中可看出絮凝沉淀处理对相对分子质量大于 1 KDa 的高分子有机物得到较好的去除,由于漂白废水中的色度主要来源于高分子氯代木素,因此色度在絮凝处理中得到了去除。废水先通过絮凝沉淀去除一部分的污染物,既保证了处理系统的稳定性,又可降低后续处理工艺的负荷。废水经厌氧处理后 COD 由 610 mg/L 降到 532 mg/L,去除率只有12%,毒性却由63%降为21%,厌氧处理后水样 COD 值中相对分子质量大于 1 KDa 的分子组分都有所增加,这可能与生物处理过程中细菌所分泌的胞外酶的絮凝作用有关。

References

[1] 宋志伟. 环境专业英语[M]. 哈尔滨:哈尔滨工业大学出版社,2005.

[2] 王黎. 环境科学与工程专业英语[M]. 北京:中国石化出版社,2012.

[3] 张一心. 环境科学与工程专业英语[M]. 呼和浩特:内蒙古大学出版社,2014.

[4] 宇德明. 科技英语阅读与写作[M]. 北京:中国铁道出版社,2002.

[5] 田学达,谭怀山,张小云. 环境科学与工程英语[M]. 北京:化学工业出版社,2002.

[6] 戴文进. 科技英语翻译理论与技巧[M]. 上海:上海外语教育出版社,2003.

[7] SONG Zhiwei, PAN Yuejun, ZHANG Kun, et al. Effect of seed sludge on characteristics and microbial community of aerobic granular sludge[J]. Journal of Environmental Sciences, 2010, 22(9): 1312-1318.

[8] CUI Daizong, LI Guofang, ZHAO Dan, et al. Microbial community structures in mixed bacterial consortia for azo dye treatment under aerobic and anaerobic conditions[J]. Journal of Hazardous Materials, 2012, 221-222: 185-192.

[9] WANG Hui, HUANG Yuming. Prussian-blue-modified iron oxide magnetic nanoparticles as effective peroxidase-like catalysts to degrade methylene blue with H_2O_2[J]. Journal of Hazardous Materials, 2011, 191: 163-169.

[10] SONG Zhiwei, REN Nanqi, ZHANG Kun, et al. Influence of temperature on the characteristics of aerobic granulation in sequencing batch airlift reactors[J]. Journal of Environmental Sciences, 2009, 21: 273-278.

[11] WEI Hui, WANG Erkang. Nanomaterials with enzyme-like characteristics (nanozymes): next-generation artificial enzymes[J]. Chem. Sov. Rev., 2013, 42: 6060-6093.

[12] PAN Yu, LI Na, MU Jianshuai, et al. Biogenic magnetic nanoparticles from *Burkholderia* sp. YN01 exhibiting intrinsic peroxidase-like activity and their applications[J]. Appl. Microbiol. Biotechnol., 2015, 99: 703-715.

[13] LU Lei, WANG Tiannv, XU Tengfei, et al. Cloning and expression of thermos-alkali-stable laccase of *Bacillus licheniformis* in Pichia pastoris and its characterization[J]. Bioresource Technology, 2013, 134: 81-86.